# PRAISE FOR
# <u>Had to Take A Break,</u>
## <u>*bicycling mis-adventures*</u>

"What a little treasure you have created.  It is so well written.  It works on several levels-bicycle travel guide for upstate New York, personal memoir, stories of courage, fear, heart break, uncontrollable joy.  I laughed out loud several times.  You have a comedian's gift and sprinkled it over the whole story."
Jackson, Australia

"Hilariously funny…Had tears running down my cheeks… My stomach hurt from laughing…Brilliantly written…I could actually visualize each story!!
Joyce, New Mexico

"…enjoyable reading…wonderful sense of humor…beautiful and entertaining illustrations"
Jackie Marchand, President, WomanTours, Rochester, New York

"I can't tell you how much I completely <u>and deeply</u> enjoyed your Book!  What a Treasure…Absolutely hilarious…as you gals were sorry to see the trips end on the last day, I was also sorry to see the story pause and finish..it was so peaceful and fun to read about your beautiful adventures.   I also loved all the personal info/history, as all of our life stories are infinitely interesting and amusing, I salute the fact of you actually being able to capture it in this book."
M. Lion-California

I loved the book and I loved the presentation. …Everyone who wants a good laugh should read it.  Anyone who's in a rut can use it for inspiration."
Amy Rivers, President of the Friends of the Library, Alamogordo, New Mexico

"it's like they said, it's not about getting from Point A to Point B, it's the journey in between, how you get there."
John Y, New Mexico (sometime bicycle rider)

*"I was up till the wee hours last night with your enchanting book.  Suuuuch* fun!"
Rhea, Denver, Colorado

**Books written by Clayton Coburn
And illustrated by Sharon Gill**


**Had to Take A Break**
*Bicycling mis-adventures*

**Had to Take** *Another* **Break**
*Bicycling mis-adventures*

# HAD TO TAKE A BREAK

*Bicycling* <sup>mis</sup> *Adventures*

**Sharon    Shannon    Clayton    Ouisi**
**1992**

**Written by Clayton Coburn**
**Illustrated by Sharon Gill**

# HAD TO TAKE A BREAK

WRITTEN BY Clayton Coburn
Illustrated by Sharon Gill

Published by
A.T. Publishing, 23 Lily Lake Road, Highland, NY 12528.
845-691-2021

Second Printing 2013

ISBN: 9780974053455

Library of Congress Control Number:   2013932278

To order additional copies of this book e-mail
coburn.clayton@gmail.com

visit our web site
www.tooomuchfun.com

# TABLE OF CONTENTS

**ROUTES**
**PROLOGUE**
**CHAPTERS**                                              Page

**EPILOGUE**

# Acknowledgment

Most of the history and information on the towns and areas we visited are from Wikipedia- the free encyclopedia, *I Love NewYork* magazine and our own experiences during our trips.
The maps of our routes are by no means accurate, but should be close enough for the reader to follow our adventures and or recreate the path for their own trips.

I would also like to say that this recount of our adventures was written from my perspective and memory which more than likely differs from the other participants. For example Sharon had no clue that we had established rules. Was she on the bike trip or what?

Lyrics used in chapter four are from Gilbert and Sullivan's Pirates of Penzance "With Cat Like Tread".

A special thanks and love to my husband Robert who not only encouraged me to see this project through but spent hours editing it.

Grazie Tony

# Dedication

This book is dedicated with love
to our children of whom we are
so proud.
Brad, Colter, Garett* and Jean.

*It is because of Garett's challenge to me that I finally put our stories in writing. Sharon and I have
had " tooo much fun" reliving our adventures.
Thank you for believing in us.

# Word from the Author

Right before the original manuscript was sent to the printers, I experienced a computer glitch which rearranged the entire manuscript of <u>Had To Take A Break</u>, Bicycling mis-adventures. In order to meet my deadline I had to send the document to the printers that day. Time was up! Panic set in and, instead of just throwing the computer out the window, I tried to correct the problem. Repeatedly I hit the control C combination to undo the error. I even called in the special ops which are headed up by my friend Marion Daross. Eventually we were able to right the document and I successfully sent it off to the printers with a huge sigh of relief. Undiscovered in my wild attempts to right the wrong, I had inadvertently undone the editing. This was only discovered after the publication.

At first I was devastated, not to mention Robert who had spent countless hours doing the editing. As time passed and I received many wonderful comments about the book, I realized that true to all the mis-adventures that surround Sharon and me, this was just one more, and how appropriate that it should occur with a book on mis-adventures. However, with this second printing, I have tried to right the errors and present the book as it was intended.

For those of you that have the first printing, be comforted in knowing you possess a limited edition of <u>Had To Take A Break,</u> guaranteed to have errors but very likely will be sought after by collectors of rare books.


Clayton

# ROUTES

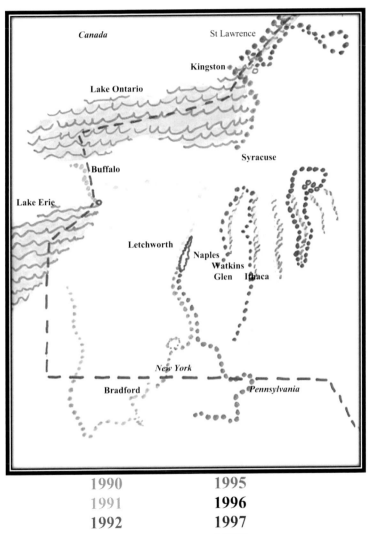

| 1990 | 1995 |
|------|------|
| 1991 | **1996** |
| 1992 | **1997** |
|      | 1998 |
| **1994** | 1999 |

Letchworth State Park, New York
1990

Shannon        Clayton        Sharon

Watkins Glen State Park
New York

Chittenango Falls State Park
New York

Grand Canyon of Pennsylvania
1992

Sharon    Clayton    Shannon    Ouisi

Wellsboro, Pennsylvania
1992

Shannon        Clayton        Ouisi

Naples, New York
1994

Clayton   Shannon   Ouisi

Niagara-on-the-Lake, Ontario

Brewster Inn    Cazenovia, New York
1996

Ouisi    Clayton    Sharon

# HAD TO TAKE A BREAK

Being an ordinary day in the summer of 1988, there was no indication that my life would take a turn. You never suspect these things, which I am sure is a good thing… otherwise why would you get out of bed? I was around forty at the time, but thinking I was twenty-two. While shopping, I happened to glance at a mirror. I distinctly remember thinking, as an older woman caught my eye, "at least I don't look that old." Then I realized I was looking at myself! Well, I was not twenty-two, nor did I look it. I also realized that I didn't feel twenty-two. It was quite a shock. Life does that to you. You go merrily on your way and then it hits you that another year has gone by….in this case almost twenty. The worst thing is that time seems to accelerate. I wonder if this could be a rarely explored consequence of Einstein's theory.

For a child, time moves like a snail…. a very slow snail. Christmas never seems to come. But as you get older, time moves a little quicker. By your twenties and thirties, time moves along at a nice pace, which is why you don't notice aging and its effects on you. By forty you are racing to keep up. Phrases such as "I don't have time…I am late," and "where does the time go?" become the normal operating phrases to get through the day and to excuse why things are not getting done.

Another interesting effect of aging is that our various age brackets carry specific topics of conversation which, of course, explains the generation gap. When I was a child the next toy was my primary focus and clothes were just something I had to put on before I could go out and play. As a teenager, nothing was worth discussing except boys, music, boys, clothes (which are now all-important), food and, of course, let's not forget boys. As a teenager I could not discuss any of these topics with anyone older than myself because it is a law of human nature that older people were never teenagers and therefore could not understand the importance and trauma created by these subjects….especially the one on boys.

In your twenties marriage, career and children were the main focus. Mothers constantly worry about how to have the smartest, healthiest and cutest child and are always on the lookout for the latest advice to accomplish these goals.

"You know you should never give your baby mashed peas."

"But I just read that mashed peas are great for sun absorption."

"Wait…that's not true….you have to read the new book on why you shouldn't feed your baby mashed peas. That book is on the best-seller list."

What an eye opener! There ensues a general stampede to the bookstore, only to find that the book has been sold-out; but a new book, *How to Teach Your Baby*

*Calculus in Two Months*, has just arrived.

By thirty a woman is either on the fast track in business or discussing, on the sideline of a soccer game, why it is so unfair that her son or daughter isn't playing.

However, once you are in your forties the reality of aging becomes more apparent. It is the location of the fountain of youth that is the main topic…and everyone has a solution.

After facing up to the passing of years, I became determined to either beat the aging process or slow it down to the previous snail's pace. Cosmetic manufacturers, diet gurus and exercise clubs love people in their forties and older. Promise me youth and vitality and I will sell my husband, child or even the dog to attain them. Besides, they are the real reason I look and feel the way I do.

The reassuring part of this revelation was that I was not alone. It is absolutely true that misery loves company. Oh, the excitement of planning the new diet and exercise program with friends! How can you not be uplifted by a phone call from a friend about a new lipstick that this time will stay on for sure? Although many have said age makes you wiser, I am afraid that this is an excuse to compensate for the loss of youth.

Cosmetics and visual enhancements are, I suppose, fine up to a point, but none of them give you vitality or the glow of a healthy body. My diet has always been fairly good, and luckily I have not had health problems. For me some sort of exercise program appeared to be the answer.

Although I grew-up in Texas, I spent a few weeks every summer near Bradford, Pennsylvania where my parents were from. Bradford is located about ninety miles due south of Buffalo, New York, nestled in the Allegheny Mountains of northwestern Pennsylvania. Settled in 1823, Bradford emerged as a wild, oil boomtown in the late 1800s. The area's crude oil has superior qualities and is excellent for refining into lubricants. World famous Kendall racing oils were produced in Bradford. The oldest continuously operating refinery in the United States, American Refining Group, is also located in this small town. The refinery celebrated its 125th anniversary in 2006. Bradford is also the home of Zippo lighters and Case knives.

During the summer weeks in Pennsylvania, I played some tennis, but never very well, so I found the game frustrating. Gyms, weight machines, aerobics and various classes were not my thing. Realistically, I knew I would never stick with any of them. Running was not an option. I never felt good when I ran and I was very suspicious of the effects the pounding and jarring would have on my body. I could not get around the thought that after a few years of running, everything from my cheeks down would settle around my ankles. Swimming was also never a consideration. There are way too many chemicals in most swimming pools, which can't be good for you. Also, swimming requires water, a commodity not always available. Walking is good. You can get caught up on all the latest gossip as you walk with friends. Whatever program I chose had to be fun or I would never stick with it. I wasn't interested in some Olympic-level training program….just something to keep me from slowly becoming a slug.

As things happened, I accidentally came upon bicycling as a solution to my quest for the vitality of youth. At the time I was at Glendorn, my family's summer home near Bradford. For some reason, which I can't begin to remember (another indication of aging), I needed to pick up something near the entry gate to the property about a mile down the road. I did not have access to a car and time was of the essence, so I borrowed one of Glendorn's Schwinn bicycles that the family kept on hand for general use. These were basic bicycles without any of today's advancements…..not a bell or whistle in sight. The bicycles did have hand brakes, but no gears, but I would not have known what to do with gears, anyway.

So, off I rode. It was incredible! I had not ridden a bike for over 15 years. The breeze all around me… seeing the countryside fly by….I just loved it. On this first outing, my destination was primarily downhill, so the harsh reality of the uphill return trip only became apparent on the way back. It didn't matter… I was hooked. I felt great…no, I felt wonderful….energized, free, and with that all-desirable adjective….YOUNG. I was a kid again! I just had to share this incredible experience.

I am one of four children, having two brothers and a sister. My sister Sharon and I have always been close. We were born one year apart and for most of our childhood we shared a room. If we omit the eight years or so when she would beat me up for no apparent reason, we have never had a fight. She apparently went through a phase where her temper would get the best of her and I was the unfortunate victim. I would make the situation worse by laughing as she was beating on me. I couldn't help it. She just looked so funny trying to pulverize me. By the time she was ten or eleven she had thankfully outgrown her bad temper.

Our Mom was an only child and both of her parents had passed away long before we were born. On the other hand, our Dad was one of six children, with a strong Irish and Scottish heritage. Exceptionally fun-loving and adventuresome, Dad and his siblings always enjoyed life, much to the chagrin of their parents. Dad was a great story teller and rarely could get through a story without tears of laughter streaming down his cheeks. Apparently this propensity for laughter was inherited by many in my family, including Sharon and me. Since laughter plays a significant role in our bicycling trips and is the greatest contributor to the "mis" in our adventures, it is important to take some time to explain this tendency. Sharon and I, along with our brothers and many of our cousins, laugh easily. We find humor in most things and events. When I laugh I do not make any sound and I stop breathing, while shaking all over. Sharon will make soft noises while stomping her feet and, at the height of a giggling episode, she will start pounding a table or anything handy. If any unsuspecting person is near I try to move them out of range.

Laughter is very contagious in our family. We all laugh and enjoy life, but when we are together there is some sort of reaction that creates an on-going series of laughter and giggle fits. Almost anything will set us off, and these fits do not always occur at appropriate times. When one of us starts, the other is pulled into the laughing vortex, regardless of where or why.

While Sharon was married to her first husband, we were rarely at Glendorn together. However, in 1988 she divorced and started planning her trips back East to coincide with mine. We both lived in Texas, I in El Paso and Sharon in San Antonio. Our parents had passed away nearly ten years before. Sharon and I not only wanted to be able to spend time together, but also wanted our children to get to know each other. I have three boys. At the time, Brad was eleven, Colter was ten and Garett, six. Sharon's daughter, Jean, was four. My husband Dick was on his fourth kidney transplant but doing remarkably well.

Immediately after my eye-opening bicycle ride, I shared my discovery with Sharon. Unfortunately, I could not consider my husband for a cycling partner. Because of surgical complications, Dick's two femoral arteries had been tied-off. Without arterial blood flow to his legs he would have had a tough time bicycling for any length of time. I could tell Sharon had doubts, but she gave it a try anyway. She took the same route I had taken and returned hooked. Throughout the remaining days at Glendorn, we would ride our bikes around the property. Soon we were joined by my cousin's daughter, Shannon, who was nineteen. Obviously she wasn't joining us to feel the exuberance of youth again…she just liked the exercise.

By the next summer we had all purchased cycling shorts, which meant we were officially bicyclists. Although we continued to bike around Glendorn on the old Schwinn clunkers, we soon found we wanted to go further.

The first time we left the property was a major breakthrough and could properly be considered the starting point of our bicycling adventures. Once we left private land we were on public roads, experiencing varying terrain and traffic. At first we were a little intimidated, but with each passing day we became more confident and would venture farther out. Without realizing it, we had fallen into a daily pattern of riding from one to two hours. We took many breaks, so I had no idea how far we were actually riding. When I did take time to figure it out, I was shocked to find that we were cycling anywhere from ten to twenty miles a day. We were so impressed with ourselves! It was about this time that one of us first brought up the idea of an overnight trip.

So began nearly twenty years of bicycling misadventures that would take us across most of New York State as well as venturing into Vermont and Pennsylvania with jaunts into Canada. Sharon and I continue our trips to this day, and each year we continue to find ourselves in funny and absurd predicaments.

Because of our budget restrictions, along with family and work responsibilities, we have only been able to take a few days each year to break away from the stress and demands of life, throw caution to the wind, and become kids again. Although our bicycling trips began as an attempt for Sharon and I to find the exuberance and vitality of youth, in the end we have found so much more. We see and experience the beautiful world God created while meeting wonderful people along the way. Our trips are just "tooo much fun," but it is the struggle of overcoming adversities and challenges that in the end give us the real joy and reward. With each journey we are blessed as our spirits are rejuvenated and life is celebrated. The following are the stories of the first ten years of our crazy journey.

**1990**
Approximately 100 miles

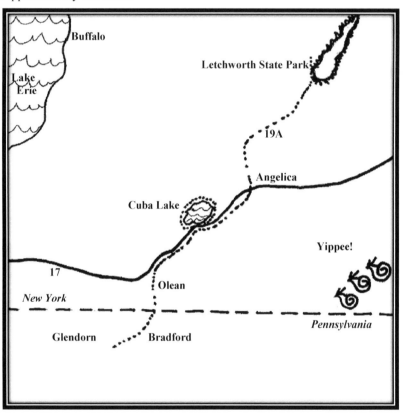

Route      •••••••••••••

Highways    _____

Chapter 1
1990

What Rules?

The decision was made. Sharon, Shannon and I were going on the road for our first overnight bike adventure...three nights, with three days of bicycling! There would be no more biking around the Bradford area within the close proximity and safety of our family. We were very excited and scared at the same time.

The planning stage took some time and, in retrospect, should have taken longer. There was so much to consider. First, we needed to be realistic about our bicycles. Riding old Schwinns in the confines of a home base was one thing, but tackling challenging terrain (our term for mountains) is quite another. It didn't matter if they were mere foothills compared to the Rockies...from our perspective they were mountains. After all, we were the ones who had to go up them! Although we were on a limited budget, Sharon and I bought new Fuji bicycles with twelve gears. Were we cool or what? Shannon, being nineteen, chose to stick with one of the old clunkers. Youth does have its advantages, which is why we were trying to recapture it.

Second, we needed to decide where we were going to bicycle. After a number of suggestions, we decided to start our trip at New York's Letchworth State Park, about 100 miles from Glendorn. Once we were dropped off at the Park, we allowed three days to find our way back. Third, before finalizing our route and decide where we would stay, we had to establish rules.

THE RULES:

    1. No riding on interstates or freeways.

    2. Ride back roads only through idyllic scenic byways, which can be hard to find since they are not always listed on maps. Wherever possible, ride along the banks of rivers and lakes. When in doubt, take the light-grey colored roads which are barely discernable on road maps.

    3. Avoid mountains, particularly at the end of the day (for us, any change in altitude could be considered a mountain). The number of hills and degree of altitude change are hard to determine using a standard road map. The exception is a skier symbol. That indicates a ski area which means high, steep mountains and not foothills. Under no circumstances attempt these areas.

    4. Plan food stops, allowing no more than five to ten miles between towns, burgs or villages.

    5. No riding in an automobile once the journey began, including going out for dinner at the end of the day.

6. No getting off our bikes to walk up a steep incline, which could be any rise in the road, but especially mountain ascents.

7. No biking at night.

8. Always wear bike helmets. By the second year we started wearing visors under our helmets to help protect our faces from the sun.

9. Always wear matching outfits. Unlike most bicyclists, we have never worn the commercially popular bicyclists' jerseys. Our "outfits" include matching oversized T-Shirts with color-coordinated bandanas to be worn around the neck, accented by the always-important matching socks. This was my rule, one of which I am exceptionally proud.

10. Stay in B&Bs. The accommodations are lovely, usually with historical significance and, most importantly, they feed you breakfast.

In writing this log, I asked Sharon to help with some of the details. When asked about the rules her answer was "what rules?" I could see right away she was not going to be any help remembering details of our adventures from twenty years ago.

Since we had to carry everything we needed for the trip on our bikes, it was important to apportion out many items to avoid duplication. For instance, we only needed one hair dryer for the three of us. We shared one tube of toothpaste and one hair brush, etc. We drew the line at sharing a toothbrush...we figured that we could handle the extra weight. Because we planned on going out in the evening, we had to allow for one evening outfit. Even with careful planning, each of our bags with our clothes, toiletries and tools weighed about 30 pounds. For our first trip, our day outfits were not as coordinated as they were to become over the years. We did, however, try to wear similar colored shirts with matching bandanas and socks.

July 31st

The first day of our adventure had arrived! Along with our gear and bicycles, we were dropped off at Letchworth State Park. As I watched the car drive off I experienced a moment of panic. In our excitement I realized we had not really thought this out. What were we thinking? There we were, three girls getting ready to take off on our own with really no clue of what we were doing. Cell phones were not readily available then and even if they had been, service would have been very limited in the area. Regardless, none of us had a cell phone so we had no way to communicate with anyone if we ran into trouble.

We had no knowledge of the road conditions and terrain. Were there shoulders to ride on, and what kind of hills where we going to face? Our treks around the Bradford area were, at most, twenty miles and we didn't carry gear.

Now we were getting ready to take on thirty miles-plus each day with 30 pounds of equipment.

Middle Falls
Letchworth State Park

Being the oldest, not to mention the instigator, I felt a sense of responsibility for the trip and the safety of my sister and cousin. There was a brief moment when

I considered suggesting that we call the whole thing off, but the sense of adventure foolishly overrode my moment of panic. As I took note of our surroundings, however, all my misgivings disappeared. Letchworth State Park is absolutely gorgeous.

The Park is located near Portageville, New York, and is named for William Pryor Letchworth, a wealthy hardware merchant from Buffalo. Letchworth came to the area in the late 1800's. In 1907 he gave the land to the state of New York on the condition that it would be preserved for public enjoyment. Within the 14,350 acre park is the Genesee River Gorge. Genesee is an Indian word for "great and beautiful." The walls of the 17 mile gorge reach up to 600 feet. As you stand on the escarpments overlooking the gorge, the heavily wooded area makes you feel that time has stood still for centuries. There are over 67 miles of designated hiking trails on the property. We spent our afternoon hiking the trails around the three waterfalls in the Gorge.

Our stay included reservations at the Glen Iris Inn. This was the family estate of William Letchworth, where they spent many summers. The Inn is a beautiful old New England home with a porch spanning the entire length of the front, furnished with comfortable wicker seating. It is located at Middle Falls which cascades 107 feet and is illuminated at night for the enjoyment of the guests. The Glen Iris was named for the ancient goddess of rainbows, inspired by the perpetual rainbow rising from the mist of Middle Falls.

That evening we wandered around the grounds and nearby trails overlooking the Genesee Gorge. We were awestruck by the sheer beauty, realizing that there is so much in this country to appreciate and experience!

While heading back to the Inn, we heard rustling in a shrub close to the trail we were on. As we watched, a bear emerged from the bushes and scampered off into the woods. We had not thought about bears and beasts on our trip. Suddenly my panic returned. What else had we overlooked?

August 1st

We really enjoyed the Inn's restaurant for both dinner and breakfast. For my morning meal I had pancakes with fresh blueberries, topped with pure New York maple syrup. Okay… it was a big breakfast, but I figured I had to "keep up my strength in these perilous times" as my Aunt B'Lee always said.

It is difficult to explain our mood that morning. It was a mixture of excitement and foreboding. At one moment we could not wait to get started, and the next we were not sure why we were doing this. We certainly wanted to prove we could, but probably more compelling was just the pure adventure of it. I had chosen not to share my specific concerns with Sharon and Shannon. It was better that only one of us was having panic attacks, although I would not have been

surprised to find out that both of my companions had similar thoughts. Well...
maybe not Sharon.

Once breakfast was finished we gathered our stuff and bungeed everything
onto the racks over the back tires. We did not own panniers and, truth be known, I
had never heard of them. Being our first bungee attempt, it took a while to get the
correct balance. Actually, it always took a while, but on this first trip we could
easily blame it on inexperience. We rode around the parking lot adjusting our bikes
and packs. Finally we were ready, but we decided to ride around the lot one more
time to be sure. Ok....no more stalling!

Off we went only to be met immediately by a rather steep hill upon exiting
the Park. Rule 6 dictated we could not get off our bikes and walk. Who thought of
this rule? As we struggled up the hill I couldn't figure out why we were even
obeying it. It couldn't be stupidity...or could it? I voted for stupidity. However, in
time all three of us made it, although Shannon making it to the top without getting
off her bike was never in question, which is more than likely the real reason Sharon
and I persevered. Neither of us was about to give in to the protests from our forty
year old bodies... not with a nineteen year old in front of us. I now understand the
meaning of the old saying "pride goes before a fall." Over

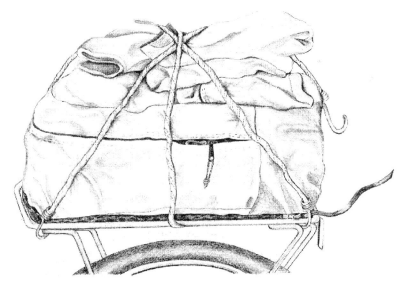

the years I have proven the validity of the saying with a number of my tumbles. However, my immediate concern was that we had only biked a quarter of a mile and had over thirty-seven to go. That small doubt as to the advisability of the trip stormed back. Sharon summed up my feelings exactly when she said, "Well, that was fun! We can go back now. Right?"

Letchworth State Park

That stop sign really meant we were supposed to turn back

Once we were out of the park the terrain became easier, which is to say it was flat, if not slightly downhill. As we cruised down the road, I was overcome by the sheer joy and exhilaration of our adventure. We were bicycling pioneers heading into the unknown and ready to take on whatever challenges were presented to us! Of course, I now realize that to be a pioneer you have to be pretty naive.

We took Route 5 down to 19A on our way to Angelica, New York, where we had reservations at the Angelica Inn. We had been biking for about three hours. No one has ever mentioned or even hinted that we are fast. In fact, we do not intend to be fast. Over the years we have never done anything to change that. We take breaks for all sorts of reasons….to take pictures, adjust gear, take a drink, get a snack, check the map, and quite a number of stops to just collapse along the side of the road for a laughing break. But whatever the excuse (all of which are legitimate) the underlining reason was to rest, particularly our buns which always seemed to be hot and sore.

As noon approached, we realized we needed to get something to eat. As we entered the next town we looked around for a pizza place. A diet high in carbs was the rage and having biked over 15 miles we were in need of lots of them, the higher the better.   During the early 1990's, villages and burgs of New York were not loaded with fast food restaurants. However, our eagle eyes spotted a pizza sign. As we were soon to learn, pizza was mostly available in bars.

Oh boy!…the place we stopped at was not a cute pub or fancy sports bar. This was a dark, grungy old place and not particularly clean. It even had a noisy screen door. I really was not sure how I felt about three ladies walking into a bar. Were we asking for trouble? Were we inviting the attention of lecherous men who hang out in these joints for just such an opportunity? I had never walked into this kind of bar before. The unknown always promotes fear, not to mention our having seen too many such movies, combined with an over-active imagination.

As it turned out, except for one occasion, this has never been a problem. I mean, really, we were not just three ladies wandering into a bar….we were three hot, dirty, sweaty ladies dressed in strange outfits having a lot of trouble walking. Combine our appearance with a few inappropriate giggles, and one could see that we were not very attractive, to say the least. A few heads might turn but that was all the attention we garnered, which was slightly disappointing but also a relief.

If you ever want a fabulous pizza with truly garden-fresh ingredients, order one in a bar in a village in upstate New York. Having biked fifteen miles added to our enjoyment. Years later we returned to that village just for the pizza.

After our delicious lunch, we were completely revived, ready and raring to go. We got back on our bikes and headed to our next destination, which was Angelica, a quaint New England village, typical of many we were to visit over the years. The town was built on Angelica Creek which feeds into the Genesee River. Angelica was the first community to be established in the Allegany County frontier lands in the early 1800's, and still retains much of its original layout.

Our reservations were at the Angelica Inn Bed and Breakfast located on Main Street. The Inn is a restored Victorian mansion and very representative of the B&Bs we were to stay in over the years. It had high ceilings, gorgeous paneling and beautiful antique furnishings, creating an ambience of years gone by. Typical of most of our B&Bs was the central staircase made of superior, highly-polished engraved wood. We loved it! Unfortunately, as our many stays in B&Bs were to prove, our rooms were upstairs…never a popular location given the weakened

27

condition of our legs. We had booked two rooms which were connected by a bathroom and an outside balcony overlooking Main Street.

As soon as we unpacked our bikes and made it to our rooms, we immediately took to our beds. After a rest, we summoned up enough energy to clean up and get ready for an evening out. We learned that the nearest place to eat was a few doors down….another bar, of course.

Being the organizer, I also had to consider all medicinal aspects of our journey. Over the years we have held to the premise that drinking a beer after arriving at our destination reduces most, if not all, soreness. It has never failed. On the contrary, if we were unable to purchase a beer, we really suffered the next day. My theory is that the beer (or beers) relaxes the muscles and helps remove lactic acid build-up. Many people may argue the point, but no one will ever convince us differently. Right or wrong, who cares…we just know it works for us.

Therefore, once at the bar/restaurant, we each ordered a beer. The legal drinking age in New York at that time was 18, so Shannon was legal. The immediate effect on our thighs was remarkable. We could feel the soreness and tightness drain from our legs. We had no idea if we could stand up, but that was not particularly important at the time.

During dinner, a couple of local men joined us. Since we really were not sure we could stand for a getaway if needed, our legs feeling akin to jelly, we ended up talking with them for some time. Now, honesty is not always the best policy. During the course of our conversation, the guys asked where we were staying. I said we were at the B&B down the street. They were very familiar with the home and one had even stayed there.

"Which room are you in?" they casually asked.

I immediately blurted out that we were in the front room overlooking the street. As soon as I finished giving our new-found friends the details of where we were staying, I received a swift kick to my shin underneath the table. I didn't feel much pain because by this time my legs were almost completely numb…. we had ordered a second beer. It never crossed my mind that ladies do not give out that much information to strange men. I was to hear about my indiscretion many times. Sometimes people, even relatives, can be so unforgiving. But when the guys started hinting that it would be fun later to sneak into our rooms, I saw the wisdom and advisability of the kick. It was time for me to shut up and for us to go, wobbly legs and all. Shannon was especially upset. She was convinced these guys would attempt to scale the wall and try to enter her room through the balcony. She spent most of the night listening for intruders, but they never came. Sharon and I, on the other hand, slept like logs.

August 2nd

We awoke early to a gorgeous day. Our legs, due to the beer therapy, were fresh, with little hint of soreness. Once we had our bags packed, we headed down to breakfast. With some apology to the many wonderful B&B's we were to stay at over the years, this breakfast has remained one of our favorites. We have never forgotten it, which is saying a lot because we have had many incredible feasts throughout the years. It was, however, one of our first B&B breakfasts. This may account for some of our enjoyment. Our hostess served us fresh berries from her garden, followed by an egg soufflé covered in cheese, with pure maple syrup poured over the top. It really was quite remarkable.

After breakfast it was time to bungee again. Once we were ready to head out, we took what was to become our traditional B&B photo, which was of us with readied bikes in front of the Bed and Breakfast. After the photo session, we headed toward Olean, New York, which was over thirty-two miles away. About half-way, we were feeling strong so we took a detour and cruised around Cuba Lake.

At one point we took a break and sat near the edge of the lake, soaking up the sounds of the water as it lapped against the shore. As the peace and tranquility slowly surrounded us, we heard a crash. Turning around we saw that all of our bikes had fallen over. Even the kickstands were unable to hold up the bicycles once the load began to shift. Obviously, we still had a lot of work to do on balancing our gear. Once again we bungeed our belongings, with even more care to keep them balanced. To be quite honest, we have never accomplished this in all our years of biking.

After crossing Route 17, we paralleled the interstate on a country road taking us to Cuba, New York. Here we stopped at the Cuba Cheese Shoppe to buy cheese and bread, along with other goodies, for a picnic we had under a nearby tree. Life was wonderful....just "tooo much fun!"

At this point Olean was still 15 miles away. We had reserved rooms in a restored Victorian home. This one was the Old Library Inn Bed and Breakfast built in 1895. We dined at the adjacent restaurant.

We were feeling very energized and admittedly a little smug after two days of biking, and felt the need for more adventures. Shannon knew of a bar with live music located in central Olean. Why did I have the feeling she had planned this ahead of time? Bicycling to the nightclub that evening was not a complete disregard of Rule # 7. Although about a mile apart, both the Library and the bar were located near the central part of town. Rule 7 states no biking at night which translates into no biking in the dark. But the streets were all well-lit. Even so, Shannon was almost hit by a car on the way. Once there, the music was great and we had a fun time. Knowing we had the "Olean Hill" the next day, we returned to our B&B early to get a good night's rest.

August 3rd

Our final day had arrived. Once again we were blessed with fabulous weather. For our last day we had a relatively short distance to ride, but we had to negotiate the Olean hill. Unlike my two companions, I had never driven to Bradford via this hill. If I'd had firsthand knowledge, I would never have planned to go that way. Rumor had it that it was a considerable, though not an excessively steep, climb. It was just long. This is a fine example of why you should never believe rumors. As we approached the hill, which I can say for a fact is a mountain, I realized how misinformed I had been. The previous days of flat terrain had given me a false sense of accomplishment and physical prowess. This was further emphasized as a bicyclist rode confidently passed Sharon and me on the way up the hill…I mean mountain. Shannon, on her old clunker, had already outdistanced us…nothing new there.

Partially to redeem ourselves, I would like to mention again that we were on 12 speed bikes weighed down by thirty pounds of gear. Now to the question… were we mice or men…uh, women? I was feeling particularly rodent-like at that moment. As we pedaled up the hill…er...mountain, I am sure Sharon and I established a new record for how slow you can pedal on a bike without falling over. Due to some sense of misplaced pride, we were hanging on to Rule 6. The tough part of this mountain was that just as we thought we could see the summit, we would soon discover that the mountain did not top-out where we had hoped but continued up…and up…and up!

After what seemed to be hours of pedaling, the end was still nowhere in sight. I feel certain that had I known the length and challenge of the ascent I would have quite intelligently broken Rule 6. Shannon would never know. I could walk faster then I was pedaling. However, I wasn't ready to quit and admit I couldn't succeed in biking up the entire mountain without getting off. It would feel like a failure, and I can be quite stubborn and unreasonable at times. Yep...Stupidity!

As I slowly ascended Olean hill, I realized how ridiculous our groans and struggles were when exiting Letchworth. In retrospect, the so called "steep hill" was more like a short incline. Well, we were certainly on a steep hill now. As never ending as it seemed, we finally reached the summit. Shannon was waiting for us at the top and was quick to inform us that the bicyclist who left Sharon and me in the dust was never able to catch her. Not only did she not get off and walk, she never raised up out of her seat to get additional leverage on her pedals for the climb. At that moment I quite honestly could not remember who had asked her to come along and saw no point in including her in any future bike trips. Admittedly, this was not a very generous thought on my part. I did cling to the knowledge that neither Sharon nor I stopped or got off our bikes during that uphill trek. So there!

The descent after the climb is what poems are written about. Few words can describe the utter exhilaration and thrill. The road down was much steeper and narrower, with many tight turns. Without a doubt, the exhaustion brought on by our long trek up gave way to total abandonment. After experiencing this downhill descent, I can understand the addictive nature that this level of thrill and adrenalin can produce. The downside is that you must survive to experience the joy and ultimate high at the bottom of the hill. In looking back there is no reason, except for God's angels watching over us, that we survived. My guess is that we traveled down the many miles of descent at about 25 miles an hour, and to add to the foolishness, we hardly used our brakes. There was enough gravel at each turn to have easily caused us to skid, lose control, and crash. In addition, the road was so narrow that if a car had been going up, there would have been little room for us to maneuver in order to avoid it, except maybe by going over the side.

At the bottom all three of us were shouting with joy. What a rush....truly incredible! I do remember getting off my bike and all of us jumping up and down and hugging with tears of joy. Would I ride the Olean hill...um...mountain down again at those speeds? No way! Am I glad I did? You bet! **

From there the road took us into Bradford where Shannon insisted that we call the family and let them know we would be arriving at Glendorn in about an hour. She was hoping for a big welcome party, which we received.

So ended our first year of our bicycling adventures. This one just whetted our appetites. We could hardly wait until next year! Was Shannon to be included even after her shameful display of athletic prowess? Did we find the fountain of youth? Of course! Of course!

**Disclaimer---Although the descent was magical, I do not recommend that anyone attempt it the way we did. There was no reason why we survived except God wanted us to go on another bike trip.

**1991**
Approximately 175 miles

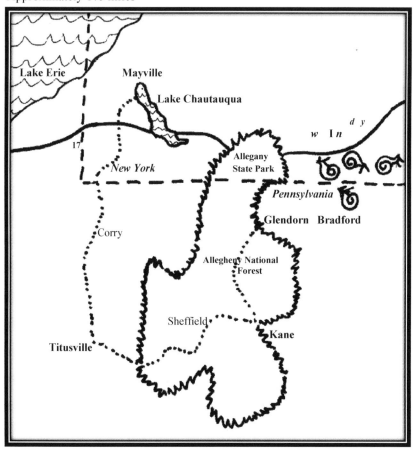

Route     ●●●●●●●●●●

Highways _____

Chapter 2
1991

Mountains, Dogs and a Hurricane

The tale of our biking adventure was met with two distinct reactions. Those who do not bike were dumb-founded and in awe of biking any distance more than a block. Experienced bicyclists would not acknowledge anyone as part of their circle unless they consistently bike double digit mileage at break-neck speeds. Since most of my friends were in the first category, our hundred mile trek was met with admiration and, in a few instances, with a small degree of envy.

Well, there were a few, mind you very few, who said they were glad it was us and not them. Many people spend their lives dreaming of adventures but are unwilling to step away from their "security blankets" to experience them. My family, by nature, are adventurous sorts. Our Irish heritage helps us find adventure and fun in all of life's experiences. My Dad always told us we could do anything we wanted in life but we must first figure out what we have to give up in order to do it.

I soon discovered that one of my dearest friends, Ouisi (Eloise) Wieland, showed a real interest in joining us. What fun! She lived in El Paso with her husband Pat. They have four boys, and the youngest two are twins and close friends of my sons. I filled Ouisi in on our route for the coming summer, assuring her we would only be cycling around thirty to forty miles a day. She was in! Sharon and Shannon were all for adding as many as would like to go, as long as they were females. We decided early-on not to include males. They would be an added complication, particularly in securing lodging. Also, they would want to be fed. However adorable males might be, including them just did not sound relaxing.

I had arrived at Glendorn a few days before Ouisi. Sharon and Shannon were already there. We spent time finalizing our plans and taking short cycling jaunts around the area. When we mapped out our route in more detail we soon discovered a small error in my estimated daily mileage. Instead of the 30 to 40 miles I had assured Ouisi, we would actually be biking more like 50 to 70 miles. Not good! This was only our second trip and we were almost doubling our daily distance from last year. I was not sure how to break the news of the longer distances to Ouisi. If she had known the true distances beforehand she might not have come. I even considered not going myself. I felt it wise to wait and tell her after I picked her up at the Buffalo airport. This gave us a two hour trip back to Glendorn for me to break the news. To soften the blow, I brought a bottle of Champagne. She took it well, but Ouisi is like that. She was game. Little did any of us know about the mountains! If we had, none of us would have gone.

For our second year, we decided to visit the Chautauqua Institute in Southwestern New York, head south into Pennsylvania to visit Titusville, travel through the Allegheny National Forest on our way to Kane, and then back to Glendorn. In order to visit the world famous institute, we chose to start our trip at Chautauqua Lake in New York.

The institute, located on Lake Chautauqua, was founded in 1874. It began as an educational center for Sunday school teachers. Currently, it is a summer retreat offering activities for all ages in the arts, including symphony, opera, theater, dance, education, religion and recreation. The 1991 summer program for the Institute included a concert by Harry Belafonte. Consequently, we planned our route and start date in order to attend his performance.

July 16th

We were dropped off at The Good Morning Country Inn, located at the southern end of Lake Chautauqua. The Inn sold all kind of gifts, including food. We first had lunch…always *the* priority. Along with Chautauqua T-shirts, we purchased facemasks, with big smiles, on a stick. The "smiley face" mask covered only the lower part of our faces. We used them often during our journey to bolster our spirits and to greet pedestrians we passed in the towns we rode through.

Once we packed our purchases onto the back of our bikes we proceeded up Route 394 to the north end of the lake to Mayville, New York. We stayed at the Village Inn B&B on Erie Street.

After we unloaded our gear and donned our evening attire, we cycled back to the Institute. As we entered the gates we were thrown back in time. Automobiles are not allowed on the grounds of the Chautauqua Institute, and it truly seemed like a time gone by. Beautiful Victorian homes line the streets which sloped down to the water. Heading for the lake, we visited a fabulous grand hotel, right out of the Great Gatsby era, where we were serenaded by violins on the veranda during afternoon tea. How wonderful not to hear automobiles, just the chatter of people as they strolled along the lakeside where water splashed against the shore. We had dinner at Webb's Captain's Table. By the way, alcohol is not served at the restaurants at Chautauqua.

Although I remember enjoying our dinner, the event that stays with us occurred while we were working out the tip. Our waiter passed by and, seeing us placing dollars on the table, immediately sat down.

"What are we playing? May I join?" he asked, and then produced several bills which he threw on the table. He was by far one of our favorite waiters, and he was pretty cute, too. We visited for a while but needed to leave in order to be on time for the concert.

Harry Belafonte was superb. We were in awe of all the different types of musical instruments that were used during the performance. What an experience and "tooo much fun!" After the show we biked the two miles uphill to our B&B in the dark. What were we thinking!? None of us had bicycle lights or reflective clothing. You would have thought that one of us would have remembered that it always gets dark at night! What was Rule 7 again? Apparently, in establishing our rules, we forgot to put someone in charge of remembering them.

"What rules?" Sharon once again asked, which instantly eliminated her from the short list for rules supervisor. Thankfully, there was little traffic and the road had wide shoulders.

July 17th

It was not until the next morning that I realized that I had left my prescription sunglasses at the restaurant. This created a major problem since I am near-sighted and very sensitive to sunlight. It was not possible for me to bicycle without them. Well, there was nothing for it but to bike back to the Institute. However it was the wrong direction, which meant we would have to bike back to Mayville to get back to our original starting point for that day, adding ten miles to an already long journey. To say the least, at that moment, I was not very popular. I quickly gave my biking pals a smiley face. They couldn't leave someone behind that shared a smiley face, could they? Besides, I had the map, so they decided that I could stay with the team…under strict probation, of course.

To make up for my mistake I studied the map in hope of finding an alternate route from the Institute to Titusville, our next B&B destination. Originally, we were to travel south from Mayville on Route 430, connecting to 76, to 474 and on to 426, then pick up 77 at Corry, which intersected 89, taking us into Titusville. It was a complicated route which reinforced the need to keep me around. On the map I found that Route 33 dropped south from the Chautauqua Institute where we could pickup Route 18. This took us east where we would connect into 430 and be back on course. Problem solved…. Not to worry…or so I thought.

To this day I am amazed that any of my biking companions still speak to me.

What is even more amazing is that they returned for the '92 trip. I cannot completely rule out mild brain damage due to the stress and over-exertion we all suffered on this trip. Ignorance is bliss, however, so off we rode with no thought to the miles we would be traveling that day, or to the unknown terrain.

After I retrieved my sunglasses, we headed down 33. The road was slightly downhill and soon all was forgiven. Our revised route couldn't be more delightful.

At the intersection of 33 and 18 we turned right, only to have our path blocked by a hill. At this point we were fresh so we plodded on slowly but surely. Once we crested the top our predicament became rather apparent. As far as we could tell Route 18 was a series of hills, one after the other. Highway 18 goes across the Alleghany Mountains, whereas our original route took us down through the valleys between mountains. According to the map, we had to travel at least six miles on 18 which meant six-plus miles of hills...up down, up down. We even had to fight off dogs. Actually, we only had a couple of dog attacks over the six-mile stretch to 430, but an attack is an attack. Dogs can be so vicious when they want to sink their teeth into your ankle. Obviously, we tried to avoid these encounters.

One in particular was quite funny...easy for me to say since I wasn't the primary victim. After three hills had been conquered we passed a farmhouse that had several dogs in the front yard. As we passed the house they came bounding out of the yard bearing down on us with great zeal. One of them was a Corgi, a small short-legged dog. We pumped our legs as fast as we could. Shannon quickly outdistanced the rest of us, including the dogs. Incredibly, I was not too far behind her. Growls and snapping teeth had caused an adrenaline rush and my legs were like pistons. Sharon was able to get away from all of the dogs except the Corgi. No matter how fast she pumped her legs she was unable to shake the critter. Every time she looked down there he was, level with her pedal. The Corgi never barked, but just kept looking up at Sharon as if to say "can we go faster?" Her inability to outdistance the little dog would have been so pathetic except we quickly remembered that we had already biked three hills....not one, not two, but three! The Corgi finally gave up. I am sure he decided Sharon and her bicycle were no challenge. We were quick to remind Sharon of her accomplishment in negotiating the three hills so that she would not be discouraged. In truth, I am not sure it helped.

So... what did we learn? Barking, snarling dogs that chase bicyclists are scary and very difficult to get past. Trying to out-distance a dog while bicycling is always a fearsome challenge. The best approach is to get off the bikes, form a tight-knit group, and slowly walk past the dogs unless, of course, you are heading down a steep hill.

Not soon enough, we connected with Route 430 and were back on our original route to Titusville. We passed through the village of Clymer, where we had something to eat at a small general store. After another ten miles, we crossed into Pennsylvania.

Snack Break

By afternoon, Ouisi was starting to have trouble with her bike. She had decided to rent one from a local dealer in Bradford instead of bringing her own. Big mistake! It was not particularly suited for long road trips and, being a rental, was not in the best of shape. The gears started to jam, which is not totally unexpected considering all the work they had to do to get up and down the hills on Route 18. It was now getting on toward evening and we still had 10 to 15 miles to go. We were already tired and hot, and now we had bike trouble. Wait... did I mention we were tired and hot?

I suddenly realized that, in our planning, we had forgotten to bring the standard bicycle tools needed to do road repairs. For instance, we did not have a patch kit or spare tube among us. What if we had a flat tire? What idiots planned this trip? It was definitely time for another smiley face.

We always appreciate angels.

Ouisi's gear problem was serious and getting worse. Every time she shifted, the gears protested until finally they no longer worked. She was stuck in one gear, which was not a problem until we had to go up a hill. Even if we had the necessary tools, I am pretty sure we would not have known what to do with them. Although Ouisi tried to push on, it became certain that we could not make Titusville before dark, or at all for that matter.

At about this time we passed a farm and saw a couple of guys working near the barn. We reluctantly decided to ask for help. This required some courage on our part because there was no way to know whether or not the men were trustworthy. It's amazing the trouble one's imagination can conjure up, but there were four of us, and they proved to be wonderful and more than helpful. They were able to get Ouisi's bike working, although with only a temporary fix. Apparently she needed some part to complete the repair. We did learn that Titusville was only about 12 miles away. Oh, so easy for them to say! The good news was that it was downhill. Yea!

Over the years we have experienced many acts of kindness and have been so grateful for each one. The Lord truly works in mysterious ways and He is there when you need Him. We know this for certain since we have needed and received help on so many occasions. Not only did these men help get Ouisi's bike in working order, but one of them showed up the next morning at our B&B with the needed part and completed the repair!

Titusville is located in a serene Pennsylvania valley. Forested hills abound with game, while Oil Creek offers a gorgeous setting for any angler. This is where it happened...."the valley that changed the world." In 1859, Edwin L. Drake drilled the world's first oil well here. In addition to the Drake Oil Well Museum and Park, there is the 7,075 acre Oil Creek State Park.

We stayed in the McMullen House on east Main St. in Titusville. After our challenging day, we were so grateful to have finally arrived. Over the years this has been a consistent reaction as we pedal up to each B&B. Our second-story rooms were up a very steep staircase. My legs almost quit. I recommended that they should, but legs can be stubborn.

July 18th

After a wonderful and uneventful night's rest we began the day with a series of stretches and exercises. For no particular reason, except possibly we are too eager to get down to breakfast, we don't do stretches anymore. Stretching is a good idea and is certainly recommended by most fitness gurus.

Breakfast was delightful! Back on our bikes, we headed out to the Drake Museum, which was very impressive. We had planned to visit Oil Creek State Park along with the Titusville Railroad, but we had 70 miles to Kane, our next evening's destination. As I glanced at my watch I saw it was nearing eleven. With the morning being taken up with stretching, breakfast, the bike repair and our visit to the museum, time had gotten away from us. Yikes...we had to get those doggies moving!

We were in the Allegheny National Forest and had to cycle up longer and higher mountains then the day before. I have considered petitioning the authorities that they rename the area Allegheny National Forest and Mountains. With a change in the name as suggested, I would have been given an important clue as to the topography of the area. I made a note for next year to get a new map.

With every tortuous uphill, we were rewarded with an exhilarating downhill. However, after each downhill we would face another uphill. Umm...I think we did this the day before! We did get a brief respite when our route took us along the Allegheny River and Tionesta Creek. This was a real treat since we were biking on level roads, thus-far a unique experience for this year's journey. The shore path did not last, so once again we were climbing mountains. Unlike Titusville, which is in a valley, Kane is on top of a mountain.

To add to our predicament, while rounding a hill we were met with such strong winds we were unable to bike forward. In fact, Sharon and Ouisi were actually pushed backwards! Apparently a category five hurricane had snuck into the area…well, it sure seemed like it.

Slowly, we made our way around the hill to find ourselves in the small town of Sheffield. We stopped at a filing station to check our tires and to come up with a new plan. We could go no further. Kane was still over 16 uphill miles away on Highway 6, and we were done-in. We had used up too much energy the day before and had nothing left after today's miles of hills, topped off with a category five hurricane.

Night was approaching. Sharon was all for sleeping at the filling station, which did not seem like a bad idea and one we strongly considered. We didn't even have enough strength to put on a smiley face, so you know our situation was serious.

Now, I cannot explain what happened next, but all of a sudden I was filled with determination, backed up by renewed energy. There is no question….I had gone "over the edge." I forcefully announced we would go forward and make it to Kane. We could not quit with the end so near, as if 16 miles from a biking standpoint is "near." Totally delusional, off I went to grab my bike. Surprisingly, everyone followed…they also were delusional. Actually, Sharon and Ouisi had drunk a Coke. The energy surge gave them enough strength to get back on their bikes. The first step was accomplished, but could any of us pedal?

As the sun descended, the air cooled and we really did experience a renewal of energy and spirit. We took one pedal stroke at a time. As Kane drew nearer, I was pedaling slowly but surely when my eye caught sight of glass shards on the shoulder ahead. Even though I saw the glass, I was unable to react in time to avoid them. I guess my surge of energy was not enough. As if in slow motion, I saw the tire go over the glass. POP! Then there was a dreaded whoosh of air escaping from the tire…my tire. So there I was, only a couple of miles from our destination, with a flat tire, without a repair kit, a pump, or an extra tube. These are such basic required items for anyone heading out on a bicycle. For any other group this would be hard to believe, but for us, well…it was becoming "par for the course."

Back to the old feet for transportation! I made yet another note to add a caveat to Rule 6. Walking or receiving a ride is allowed when your bike is broken or you have flat tire. Shannon went on ahead…actually, she was always ahead…to find help. Sharon and Ouisi stayed with me for moral support. In other words, they couldn't keep up with Shannon. Besides, they did not want me to be alone. After getting them into this fix, I thought their support was very generous. On the other hand, I still had the map.

Shannon returned with a pickup and a driver. What a gal! I loaded my bike into the back. Sharon and Ouisi, who had only an hour before been reduced to tears through sheer exhaustion complicated by the category five hurricane, were now the model of determination and chose to bike on. What style!

Our hero in the pickup took Shannon and me to a filling station where a couple of the attendants fixed my tire. Back on our bicycles, we soon joined Sharon and Ouisi at the Kane Manor Country Inn.

The Kane Manor was built for Dr. Elizabeth Kane, who named it Anoatok. The name came from an Inuit Eskimo word for "wind loved spot." The manor is a turn-of-the-twentieth century national and historical landmark. When we were there this magnificent Inn needed a lot of tender loving care. However, the staircase was gorgeous, slightly curving up to the second floor where, once again, we were to stay. Our legs were so numb they had no clue that they carried us and our gear up the stairs to our room. I am sure we ate something somewhere but the fog of exhaustion that day has concealed what and where.

July 19th

As the sun rose on our final day we were greeted with an incredible view. We were on top of a mountain, hence the name chosen by Dr. Kane. Looking around, we saw a series of mountain ranges, some of which we had been cycling for two days. We celebrated this glorious morning with joy and thanksgiving. Ahead was a ten mile downhill ride taking us down to Corydon Street near the entrance to Glendorn.

Life seemed incredible! We were grateful for our journey which gave us some tough challenges while we experienced a wondrous countryside. Along the way we were blessed by wonderful, caring people who took time to offer their help when we had nowhere else to turn. Without any of us saying a thing, we all reached for our smiley faces. How soon the physical torture from miles of hills, emotional trauma of attack dogs, broken gears, flat tires and a category five hurricane were forgotten!

**1992**
Approximately 160 miles

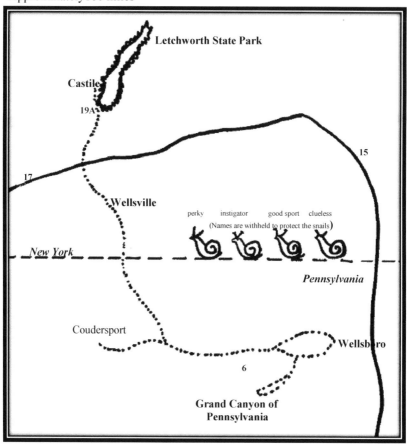

Route  ● ● ● ● ● ● ● ● ● ● ●

Highways  ─────────

Chapter 3
1992

Balloons, Bears, and Snails

Sharon, Shannon, Ouisi and I were back for another adventure. After last year's tour, it would not have surprised anyone if we had called it quits. However, several factors persuaded us to continue for another year:
1. Last year's thrilling ten mile downhill on the final day.
2. The gala celebration upon our return. At the time there were around forty aunts, uncles and cousins, along with friends, staying at Glendorn. Everyone turned out to cheer and wave flags when we returned. The younger cousins had made special T-shirts, and the four of us were treated to massages. To complete the celebration a welcome-back dinner had been planned. Tooo much fun!
3. I had to guarantee a less challenging tour. No more Allegheny Mountains or category five hurricanes.....some people have no sense of adventure.
4. The most persuasive argument was that we just loved the adventure and camaraderie. With all the demands and stress of everyday life, we had to take a break. It's so simple really.....just jump on a bicycle and be a kid again. Besides, last year's challenges had made us tougher and bonded us as a team. All for one and one for all!

In planning this year's trip, we decided to return to Letchworth State Park in New York. We knew some of the area and, more importantly, we knew the terrain. For us, the important words were *flat* roads and *fewer* miles. But instead of planning a route that would bring us back to Glendorn, we arranged to be picked up near Coudersport, Pa. which allowed us to include a visit to the Grand Canyon of Pennsylvania.

July 15th
On a gorgeous midsummer day we were once again dropped off at the Glen Iris Inn. We had reserved two adjoining rooms which, of course, were located on the third floor. After we settled in, we still had plenty of time to explore and show

Ouisi why we were so eager to share this area of New York with her. We decided

Letchworth State Park

Very high trestle over the Genesee River

to hike along the Genesee River to the Upper Falls. The path begins at the spectacular Middle Falls which is near the Inn. The Upper Falls are not as wide or as tall as the Middle Falls, but are just as beautiful. The path wound its way along the rim of the Genesee Gorge through verdant woodlands where, if we had not been chatting so loudly while watching the flow of the river, we probably could have seen Leprechauns peeking at us from behind moss covered rocks.

Just above the Upper Falls is an old wooden railway trestle spanning the river. We were told that it is the highest trestle of its kind still in use. Our trail took us up to the rail bed. Once we reached the track, Shannon was determined to venture out onto the trestle. Being incredibly intelligent in these matters, and realizing that someone needed to stay back to notify her next of kin, I volunteered to watch her attempt to cross the extremely high trestle. Ouisi and Sharon could see that I would need help of some kind, so they stayed with me. Once the Evel Knievel-like daredevil came back to safety, the four of us returned to the Inn where we enjoyed a scrumptious meal, complimented by a fine New York Wine.

July 16th

Our rooms were delightful. Shannon and Ouisi were in one room, while Sharon and I shared the other.

The next morning we awoke to sounds coming from right outside our window, which I could have understood if our rooms had been on the first floor. I distinctly remembered, however, that we were on the third floor. As Sharon and I tried to make sense of the voices and heavy footsteps, Shannon tore into our room. She could barely speak. We were obviously under attack! We jumped out of bed, hardly touching the floor, in order to save ourselves. As we threw on our clothes we noticed Shannon peering out of the curtains. Before we could get a report of the impending disaster she flew back into her room. We quickly followed. As we entered the room we found Shannon with her back against the wall peering around the curtain. This, of course, is the best position to take to see danger coming while not giving away your position. Sharon and I immediately threw ourselves against the wall. Ouisi was not to be found. She had obviously locked herself in the bathroom. Smart....very smart!

Once in position against the wall, I realized there was a roof to a two-story extension right outside our windows. It took only a few more minutes before we realized that the noise was coming from workers repairing something on the roof. Now, this was not exactly the proper time for repairs, as it was only about 7:30 a.m., but hardly cause for the panic Shannon had exhibited.

Then I saw him! Shannon was not panicking...she was gaga. One of the workers was one of the most gorgeous males any of us had ever seen. Decked out in his blue jeans and adorned with his tool belt, it was very hard to keep our eyes off of him. Although we were all very appreciative of his good looks and stature, Shannon, being young and attractive, was the only one determined to find an excuse to meet him. I didn't blame her. The rest of us left Shannon tearing from room to room while we went down for breakfast. Later we found her outside working on her bike trying very hard to get Mr. Adonis' attention. Where there is a Shannon, there is a way! As it turned out she was able to have a brief conversation with him, only to have to part as we rode off into the sunrise. Now, where were we going and why? I mean he really was very handsome. We left Letchworth with an even greater appreciation of all of God's creations.

Our route called for a forty-mile ride to Wellsville, New York, along Highway 19. Upon reviewing the map, I was particularly pleased to see that there was not a skier symbol in sight. They are easy to miss because they are very small. In route, we planned to return to the same bar where, two years before, we had enjoyed that fabulous home-made pizza. The bar had not changed, the pizza was just as delicious, and we were still the same hot, dirty, sweaty ladies in strange outfits, except now there were four of us. I cannot be sure, but I do believe the men at the bar were the same ones we had seen two years before. We also attracted about the same amount of attention as we had during our first visit.

Our Bed and Breakfast was located in Scio, New York, just north of Wellsville. Due to our delayed start out of Letchworth, we didn't arrive until late afternoon. Scio was so small we had little to choose from for an evening meal. There was a bar which advertised food, but it was too rowdy and full of tobacco smoke. Across the street was a convenience store. We purchased our medicinal beer along with some sandwiches which we took back to the B&B.

July 17th

By now we had our morning routine down. We'd pack up our gear, walk (no running) to breakfast, where we always ate too much with no regrets. After we bungeed our gear onto our bikes, we had a group photo taken in front of our B&B. Our next stop was sixty miles away in Wellsboro, Pennsylvania.

We rode south on 19 through Wellsville, New York. The area was first settled in the 1800's and named for Gardiner Wells, one of the first settlers to arrive there. It was in Wellsville that we made *THE* purchase that, years later, would play a significant role in one of our most popular stories. Knowing that we needed to add to our outfits, we purchased four hot-pink T-shirts depicting the annual

Wellsville hot air balloon festival.

In addition to purchasing T-shirts during our travels, we also, over the years, bought pins from the areas we visited. Sharon was the only one of us to figure out a way to display our ever-growing pin collection. She placed them in the clear pouch of a small carrier strapped to the front of her bike. If anyone had taken the time to look over our collection, I have no doubt they would have been impressed by the varied symbols of our extensive travels.

With our purchases successfully bungeed to the ever-increasing stack of stuff on the back of our bikes, we headed for Wellsboro, where we had reservations at the Four Winds Bed and Breakfast. Our trip took us through the Black Forest where we delighted in the beautiful, long-needle pines.

Leaving the Black Forest, we turned off 449 onto Highway 6. The weather had been threatening all day as dark clouds continued to build. With over thirty miles to go to Wellsboro, the rains began, quickly increasing into a torrential downpour. Wet!....I mean we were really wet! I am convinced we could not have been any wetter. Not only were we drenched by the rain, but each passing vehicle covered us anew with water. It was like pedaling through small waterfalls. At first we were miserable as water trickled down our backs and front. However, once the water reached my socks and shoes and I was completely soaked, the rain did not seem to bother me. Our rain gear was worthless. Actually, I'm not sure we had rain gear, which is probably why it didn't help.

Upon arriving at our B&B I was relieved that our hosts, Debbie and Charles Keister (bless their souls), not only welcomed us, but also offered us their clothes dryer. I would not have blamed them if they had turned us away since we looked like nothing short of drowned rats. To be truthful, we looked worse. Over the years we have found that, with few exceptions, the hosts and innkeepers of B&Bs are warm, caring folks who welcome us as if we were family.

What a day we'd had and what important lessons we had learned:
1. Always carry bright rain gear. Camouflage or dark greens are poor choices while biking on the shoulder of a road. Not only is it hard for the drivers of vehicles to see you, but it is also hard to see each other. Let me be clear here. The rain gear is not just to keep you dry. It is also to keep you visible.

2. Additional reasons to always stay in B&B's. They do not mind that you look like drowned rats. They still let you stay there. They have dryers to dry you, your clothes, and your shoes.
3. Always put your gear in a heavy-duty garbage sack (black is a nice choice) or if you are concerned about looks, place your gear in a garbage sack and then shove the whole thing into your bag (we still did not know about panniers).

Wellsboro is a charming turn-of-the-century borough and the Tioga County Seat. Founded in 1806 by settlers from Delaware, Maryland and Philadelphia, the town was named in honor of Mary Wells, wife of one of the original settlers, Benjamin Wister Morris. The Borough has been placed in the National Register of Historic Places. There are over 600 properties deemed worthy of preservation.

The Fair Winds B&B is right off Main Street. Although the storm had moved on, the seats of our bicycles were still wet. To avoid getting our bottoms wet, we elected to walk into town. Wait…what happened to rule five? In unison, we all echoed Sharon's thoughts, "what rules?"

We strolled along the Main Street Boulevard. Having read about the streets lined with maples, grand elm trees, and gas lamps, we wanted to experience its ambience as well as the history.

We ate at The Steak House, which had been recommended to us. Having survived the torrential rains, we were ready for a quiet meal in a cozy, warm restaurant. We are always starved while on our trips, and surviving torrential rains while biking is an acceptable excuse to feast. And feast we did!

Sharon in particular was feeling the effects of our watery adventure. She was tired and hungry. Because she usually does not eat red meat, the rest of us felt that she was protein deprived. Consequently, we all encouraged her to up her protein intake. One needs energy to bike, and protein to repair well-used muscles. Although not a rule, we would hate to get into a habit of leaving fellow bicyclists behind. If, under extreme circumstances, it did become necessary to abandon one of us, I am sure we would do our best to remember where we last saw her. However, there were no guarantees. Once Sharon became aware of her predicament, she chowed down. We followed our meal with a scrumptious desert. Full and satisfied, we meandered back to our B&B.

July 18th

The next morning we awoke to an incredible day. Full of energy, we quickly finished another fabulous breakfast and headed out to begin a new day. Isn't it wonderful how all of our breakfasts were fabulous? That's a B&B for you!

Fresh rain-washed air filled with the sounds of birds greeted us as we stepped outside. We just wanted to hug ourselves for being alive to enjoy this halcyon day. The early morning we spent in Wellsboro was a trip back in time, filled with a gentleness and a beauty of by-gone days. As we headed out under the canopy of trees, we experienced a true love and joy of our biking journeys. Our spirits just soared! A couple of us burst into song out of pure happiness. That we had just blasted out with song was a great shock to the birds that were doing a beautiful job of greeting the morning, but we couldn't help it. I have no doubt they recovered as we put distance between ourselves and the town.

Our euphoria was slightly marred by the knowledge that this was our last day. I remember feeling strong, and I really regretted that our adventure was to end so soon. We all were having "tooo much fun!" We did, however, have a wonderful day planned, so off we rode to Leonard Harrison State Park, home of the Grand Canyon of Pennsylvania.

I have not only been to Arizona's Grand Canyon, but I have also hiked to the floor and back. It was difficult envisioning what Pennsylvania's Grand Canyon would be like. I did expect something less than the Arizona Grand Canyon, since Pennsylvania's canyon had not made the eight wonders of the world list.

Our ride to the entrance was about 18 miles. There was little traffic and the terrain was about right for casual cycling. The entrance to Leonard Harrison State Park is along Route 660. From there the Grand Canyon continues south for about forty-seven miles. The canyon was formed when the Laurentide Continental Glacier moved into the area. The deepest point at Pine Creek Gorge is 1450 feet, and the canyon is one mile wide. The movement of the glacier into the area changed the course of Pine Creek from a northeasterly flow to its current southerly direction. In 1992, Pine Creek was designated a Pennsylvania Scenic River. The banks are lined with a large abundance of deciduous hardwood trees displaying a panorama of colors in the fall. Sprinkled among the deciduous trees are several varieties of pines.

The overlook was located down a rather steep hill. Down is never a problem, except in this case the enjoyment of the descent was marred by the realization that we would have to come back up. There was something familiar about that scenario. As we rode down I made a mental note to check if there was an alternate exit.

After leaving our bikes in the parking lot, we walked to the lookout. The view was beautiful but it was not a "grand canyon" as defined by Arizona's Grand Canyon. Try as we might, it was difficult not to compare this canyon (quite unfairly) to the stupendous one we were familiar with out west. Our reaction was, "where is it?" From our vantage point there weren't the miles of sheer rock walls descending thousands of feet to the Colorado River, which gives the Grand Canyon of Arizona its spectacular appearance. Time did not allow us to hike part of the Pine Creek Trail which, I understand, is well worth the trip. Another day perhaps.

Upon approaching our bicycles, we heard a loud roar. As the roar increased in volume, the first of many motorcycles appeared on the road, heading towards the overlook. This group definitely could have come out of MGM central casting. All the motorcyclists wore dark leather and many had the regulation beard and tattoos. Several riders had similarly dressed women holding on to them. As a group, they looked pretty scary and I was glad to be leaving. With barely a nod, we quickly mounted our bikes and rode off.

The lookout was at the end of the road, so there was no alternate exit. Rats! Once out of the parking area, we did our best to make it up the hill with our 30lb. loads. We were still determined to adhere to Rule 6. Why we felt we had to follow this rule when so many of our other rules had been discarded was beyond me. As snails passed us on the way up the road, the absurdity of Rule 6 became crystal clear. Who thought of these rules? Of course, according to Sharon, we didn't have any rules.

After managing about 20 yards, Shannon had to quit. Her back had started to spasm. Why hadn't I thought of that? Seriously, she could go no further. About this time, a pickup truck went by. Recognizing that we had a problem (nothing new there), the driver stopped to ask if he could help. We loaded up Shannon and her bike and planned to meet her at the entrance, which was conveniently located at the top of the hill. I had generously offered to keep her company but she insisted it was not necessary. Double rats!

The rest of us continued the ascent, which had unfortunately become steeper while we had paused to help Shannon. It was next to impossible to get our bicycles moving from a complete stop on a steep hill. The weight of our gear and its precarious positioning caused the bicycles to fall to one side unless we were able to pedal fast enough to maintain our balance. Instead of trying to get our bikes moving from a dead stop on the steep incline, we had to turn around and go back down to get enough speed to go up the hill. Even then it was a challenge for us. After several attempts, we all managed to get our bicycles moving in the right direction. Foot-by-foot, inch-by-inch we made our way to the top where we were greeted by a group of snails that was cheering us on.

Not far from the entrance and at the top of our "Mount Everest" was a convenience store. In front of the store, on the other side of a split-rail fence that ran along the road, was a tree with such a large inviting canopy, we couldn't resist. Although Shannon was further up the road at the entrance, we had to take a break. After grabbing our water bottles and snack packs, we assembled under the tree in a semi-circle facing the trunk with our backs to the road.

Without any warning a piece of candy fell from the tree. Now, you do not expect this sort of thing, so we all just looked at it lying on the ground. Most likely we were all suffering from delusions, complicated by possible mild hypothermia brought on by the extreme exertion of having just climbed a mountain. As we continued to stare at the fallen candy, another piece fell next to it and was quickly followed by another and then another. The Grand Canyon of Pennsylvania may not be one of the eight wonders of the world but this tree sure should have been. As a few more pieces rained down on us, Sharon, who was the first in line, slowly turned and let out a yelp. Her yelp was followed by a gasp as Ouisi, next to her,

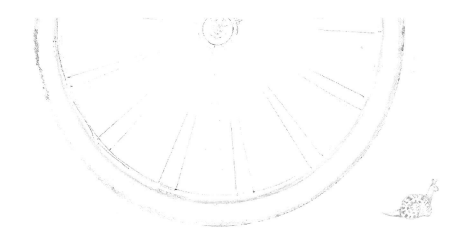

turned to see what had startled Sharon. I followed with a sharp intake of air as I turned to see what was going on. The exclamations were repeated in the same order a second time before we could deal with what appeared behind us. A bear was lofting candy at us. The sight was beyond words. It actually took us a few moments to register that this was someone in a bear costume. We then just collapsed in laughter. So many emotions had to be dealt with in such a short span of time….curiosity as to why candy had fallen from the tree, followed by a stab of fear at seeing a bear, which culminated in comic relief when we recognized that the candy thrower was a person in a bear costume.

Once we were able to stand up, we went over to our new friend and received a gentle hug plus more candy. As I received my hug, out of the corner of my eye, I saw what appeared to be snails rolling on the ground with laughter. Nah….couldn't be! I am sure I must have been mistaken. I quickly turned to Sharon and Ouisi, only to see that they were already heading out of the Park to find Shannon. Ignoring the snails, I told our buddy the bear goodbye. He was not to be the last friend we were to make that day.

At the entrance we joined Shannon, who seemed to have recovered. That made one of us. Although by this time we had overcome our exhaustion from our uphill trek, we were still a little shaky from being passed up by snails and having candy thrown at us by a bear. After taking a vote, Sharon, Ouisi and I decided there were some things Shannon need not know.

We returned to US 6 by route 362. Once on 362 we saw what was to become our favorite highway sign. The sign warns truckers of a steep downhill ahead. Yippee!!! Off we pedaled with renewed energy, reaching speeds of up to 30 miles an hour. The snails had no chance. We were flying! That downhill was several miles long. Tooo much fun!

All too soon, the road leveled out.  As we passed a large Victorian home on the left that had been converted into a bar. As one, we all yelled "PIZZA"
and immediately turned into the parking lot. We had to take a break! As we entered

Our new buddy

the bar, I saw the ladies room directly in front of me. I headed in that direction while the others ordered the pizza.

Within a minute there was a rap on the door. Apparently there was a problem. On exiting the ladies room I immediately looked for snails. The bartender had informed the others that thirty-plus motorcyclists were due to arrive any minute. The owner felt he needed to give us a heads up that we were soon to be engulfed by a "motorcycle gang." Great! Now what? Since hunger overruled common sense, we stayed. This had to be the same "gang" we had seen at the Grand Canyon Overlook.

Once again panic set in. I always felt that the safety of our group fell on my shoulders. As much as I would like to resign from that position, no one has stepped forward to replace me. My mind was whirling with various scenarios, all of which had been depicted in the movies. What if they were looking for young girls to forcibly join their gang? Shannon was of course the most likely candidate. As I was mentally composing a letter to inform her parents that their daughter had been abducted by a motorcycle gang, the familiar sound of motorcycle engines filled the bar. In they came. As soon as they saw us one of the "gang members" came over. Well that was it. There was no way Sharon, Ouisi and I could save Shannon.

More new buddies

However instead of grabbing Shannon, he looked at all of us in disbelief. He could not believe we had made it so quickly from the overlook to our current location. He was completely dumbfounded. After all, we were on bicycles and they were on motorcycles.

Although we were not aware that there had been a race, we were secretly proud of the fact that we had beaten them to the bar. Soon several more riders joined us at our table. As it turned out they were a group of businessmen who, on behalf of Harley Davidson, ride their motorcycles around the countryside. In addition to promoting Harleys, they help raise money for a children's hospital.

I learned an important lesson that day.....never to prejudge people, and to get a hold of my imagination, for gosh sakes! I could forget about the letter to Shannon's parents. We actually had a fun time talking with these guys. We debated the merits of motorcycles vs. bicycles, but from our point of view there was no contest.

They were very interested in our trip and what we were doing. I made sure to steer the conversation away from snails and bears. Soon it was time for us to head out. Before we parted, Shannon took a short ride in the parking lot on one of the motorcycles.

We had planned to end our journey near Coudersport, Pennsylvania, where we had arranged to be picked up for our return to Glendorn. With over thirty miles to go, but on flat roads, we headed off. It didn't take long before several of the motorcyclists passed us. As each went by we were greeted with honks and waves. They were strung out for miles, so the honks and waves continued for over an hour. It gave us a warm feeling to know we had friends on the road.

After we had been picked up in Coudersport, ending that year's journey, we passed the motorcycles parked in front of another bar and were tempted to stop for a visit. However, we felt we would lose a little credibility arriving in a car.
"Tooo much fun"!

**1993**
Approximately 150 miles

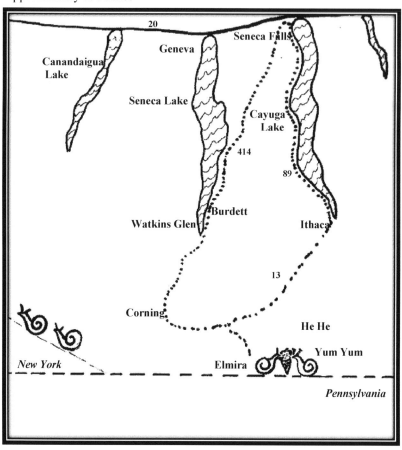

Route ••••••••••••

Highway _____

Chapter 4
1993

The Hand of God

With another year gone by, all of us were eager and excited for our break from the everyday demands of life. By 1993 all of Ouisi's boys were teenagers, and two out of my three boys had also reached those critical years. Sharon, a single mom with a nine-year-old daughter, was always ready for a break, while Shannon looked forward to some time away from her college studies.

Although we had attended Harry Belafonte's concert two years before, during this fourth year we officially began our cultural phase. Our tours were not only about bicycling to a destination, but also about experiencing the journey. We were biking through incredibly beautiful country steeped in history, so we wanted to take more time to explore the areas while enjoying their festivals and activities.

The first step in planning our trip was to decide on the region we wanted to explore. Next, we would locate B&Bs within a two hundred mile radius that were not located near a skier symbol on the map. We then researched the region to find annual events and historical sites, along with nature preserves and parks. In addition, we scheduled more evening activities into our adventures (as if biking is not adventure enough). The final route was determined by linking the towns together in a way that allowed for about forty miles between the B&Bs, while taking in as many sites and events as time would allow.

We also added to our choices of daytime bicycling outfits. For the first time, we would all be properly coordinated. During the preceding winter Sharon decided to purchase a new bike, one with twenty-one gears. What a wimp! The rest of us were purists and continued to use our physically challenging 12 speed bikes. What idiots!

With the new plan in place, we choose to begin an exploration of the Finger Lake Region located in west-central New York. The Finger Lakes are a result of glacial movements from two different Ice Ages. As the glaciers moved through the area, they gouged out miles of dirt and rock, leaving behind long, narrow lakes which appear to form the fingers of a hand. Legend suggests that the Creator looked upon the region with special favor, and in reaching out to bless the land, He left behind the imprint of His hand.

The Finger Lakes area is comprised of numerous deep gorges with rushing waterfalls combined with fertile, wide valleys creating topographical marvels found nowhere else in the world.

Our journey started at Elmira, New York. Settlers moved into the Elmira area circa 1788. Historically, the town derived its name from a child that wandered into a meeting being held by local politicians who had gathered specifically to decide on a name. Elmira is best known as the summer home of Samuel Clemens, alias Mark Twain, who married Olivia Langdon, a local girl. Thereafter the family spent their summers near Elmira, and it was here that Clemens wrote *The Adventures of Huckleberry Finn*.

July 18th

A friend of Sharon's drove us to Elmira where we were dropped off at the Lindenwald House, which is over 125 years old and still operating as an Inn. At the time of our stay, Sharon and Michael Dowd, our Innkeepers, were in the process of renovating the forty-four room Italianate mansion.

We were all looking forward to our evening out. Since this was the summer home of Samuel Clemens, each year the Mark Twain Musical Drama was held at the Elmira Murray Athletic Center. The center is just outside of town, a couple of miles from our B&B. On the way out we stopped at Pippins for something to eat before the show.

As we took our seats, a woman behind us asked how far we had traveled on our bicycles. I was surprised by her question, since we had donned evening attire. How could she know we had been bicycling? Of course…we still wore helmets and had carried them into the Center! She proceeded to tell us about her sister who for years suffered from tremendous back pain. Her sister's doctor had recommended that she take up bicycling. Not only did bicycling relieve her pain, she became totally taken with the sport. According to her sister, she had already biked coast to coast, Atlantic to Pacific, and was currently biking throughout Europe. Not forgetting this success story, I have passed it on to others who suffer from chronic back pain in hopes that it might be of help.

The show was great fun and we enjoyed it very much. After the program we headed outside to get on our bikes for our journey back to the Lindenwald.

OOPS….while we were watching the show it had become dark outside. This should not have been a surprise, as we had experienced this nightly phenomenon after the Harry Belafonte concert. How do we forget such details? Obviously we still did not have a rule enforcer. Fortunately Shannon did have a light on the front of her bike. Even though it was small and not very bright, it worked. We decided the best plan was to follow Shannon as she would light the way, and try to stay close together in order to appear to be a large obstacle that we hoped cars would want to avoid. With so much traffic whizzing by us we were all pretty terrified, to say the least. Even if we were not hit by a car, one or two of us would more than likely suffer a heart seizure. There was no question….this was one of our stupidest moments.

We arrived back at the Lindenwald safely, probably surrounded by a host of angels. Immediately, all of us put on our "must not leave home without it" list large headlights, tail lights and reflectors, not only for the bikes but also for ourselves. Pulsating lights are also a particularly nice and effective safety addition for the sides and rear of a bicycle.

July 19th

After breakfast, of which, amazingly, I have no memory, we headed out of town. That was a challenge in itself. Elmira was not one of the small, quaint towns we were accustomed to touring. There was a fair amount of traffic and we had to get across Highway 17 to reach Farm Road 13, which took us into Ithaca, New York, the home of Cornell University. Our route was only a little over 30 miles, although we did have a slight incline.

Once out of town and away from all the traffic, we leisurely biked along the pristine forested country road. Not long after we started along 13 we came across a farmers market. We had to take a break! We just love these markets because we always find wonderful local goodies, such as fudge, to munch on. Because I do not eat chocolate, I always went for the maple fudge, while the others indulged in all varieties of chocolate. Yum!

After the delicious break, we continued on to Ithaca, which was named for the Greek Island of Ithaca. The city is located on the southern shore of Cayuga Lake. When the Europeans first arrived, the area was home to the Saponi and Tutelo Indians who were part of the Iroquois confederation. With the destruction of the confederation's power, the tribes were driven from the area. Most local land titles go back to Revolutionary War grants. Ithaca is nationally known for the Ithaca Gun Company, makers of highly-valued shotguns, and Ithaca Calendar Clocks. During the 20$^{th}$ century the city was an important center in the silent film industry.

Before entering the town, we stopped at the lower part of Buttermilk Falls State Park, named for the foaming cascade formed by Buttermilk Creek as it flows down the steep side of the valley towards Cayuga Lake.

That night we stayed at the Peregrine House located in downtown Ithaca. It is a lovely, small Victorian B&B. Once again we donned our evening clothes for our reservations for a dinner cruise on Cayuga Lake. What a pleasure to drift along the banks of the lake, enjoying spectacular views while being served a lovely meal. We were now getting the hang of planning our bike tours. After a wonderfully relaxing cruise, we headed back to our B&B. It was still light, so we did not have to experience the terror of biking in the dark in heavy traffic. This was not something any of us wished to repeat.

July 20th

Another gorgeous morning had arrived. Our original plan was to bike around Cornell before heading up the west side of Cayuga Lake on our way to Seneca Falls, about fifty miles to the north. Once we discovered that Cornell was built on top of a hill (as you know by now, hills are always interpreted by us to be close cousins to mountains), we decided to forego touring the University. Ithaca is a large town, so we had more traffic then we were comfortable with. Any town with more than one stop light was really too big for our liking. Might as well admit it ...cars intimidate us. Hey, they're bigger and tougher then we are!

As we headed out of Ithaca we had our first accident in our four years of bicycling. Ouisi somehow caught her wheel on a curb trying to cross a busy intersection and down she went. Other than a pretty nasty scrape on her knee and being a little shook-up, she was okay. Once we re-bungeed everything back onto her bike we eagerly left busy Ithaca behind us. Country roads are more our style.

We biked along Farm Road 89 that hugs the coastline of Cayuga Lake, the second largest of the Finger Lakes. Throughout most of the day our view of the lake was blocked by the dense forest of deciduous trees.

By early afternoon we caught sight of a small village down by the water. We had to take a break. Being eager to stroll along the lake, we did not take into account the consequences of the "down" part of getting there. As mentioned, the Finger Lakes were formed by glaciers gouging out canyons and gorges as they moved through the region. As the ice moved south, hills were formed as dirt and rock piled up on each side with the hills became increasingly higher the further south the ice moved. The spot where we decided to drop down was about halfway to Seneca Falls, so it was not the highest section of hills, but the road was still very steep.

The shore-side village was so charming. Most of the homes and stores are right on the lake, and the entire village is only a few blocks long. We enjoyed strolling along the sidewalks while stopping to poke our heads into a few stores. We had a make-shift picnic on one of the boat docks at the shore. Towards the north end of the village we discovered an ice cream parlor. Well….what can I say? Having biked for several hours, none of us could resist.

Once we purchased our treats we retired to rocking chairs on the porch of the ice cream parlor. We sat enjoying the view of the lake as it stretched out in front until it was corralled by the tree covered hill on the opposite side. The only discernable noises, other than the water brushing up against the shore, were the slurps of us downing the ice cream, coupled with the creaking of the chairs. The serenity was so enticing that we were unaware of how much time had passed. Someone, whose identity has long since been forgotten, broke the spell and mentioned we probably should think about heading out. Reluctantly, we knew we had to continue. Time was passing and we were barely halfway to our destination.

As we turned west to head out of town we were met with a wall, also known as a very steep hill that went on forever. It was about this time that the effects of the ice cream hit Sharon and I. The combination of the "wall" and the ice cream was disastrous. For some reason, certainly unknown to us and probably only to be determined by years of research, Sharon and I start to laugh after we eat ice cream. This is not just a giggle, but an entire body shaking, no-breathing laughter. For our part, we have never needed to understand why…it just happens.

Both of us hesitated briefly before ordering our ice cream, but decided to overlook this potential consequence. Besides, the giggle fits do not occur every time, and we wanted the ice cream. We did mention this possibility to Shannon and Ouisi but they shrugged it off as ridiculous, although Shannon, as part of our family, did give pause.

What a predicament…we had to scale the wall, which had to be accomplished hauling over 30 lbs. of gear, our stomachs sated with ice cream, while being unable to breathe due to our laughter. The combination just didn't work, so there was only one thing to do.

Sharon and I got off our bikes and, being unable to stand, laid down on the side of the road while clutching our stomachs in hilarity. Since there is no way of knowing how long one of these fits will last, we motioned for Shannon and Ouisi to save themselves and go on. It did enter my mind that I hoped one of them would think to send someone back to locate the bodies if we did not show up in a few days. Time and many miles were against us. Sharon and I are proof that "dying of laughter" can be a distinct possibility. The fastest way for us to get past one of these fits is not to look at each other, since once we make eye contact we start laughing all over again.

Shannon and Ouisi left us on the side of the road. What else could they do? They knew that it would be some time before we would be able to get back on our bikes. Like the aftershocks of an earthquake, we always have follow-up giggles. Once we were able to breathe again, we attempted to mount our bikes, only to be overcome by another laughing fit. We were facing a worse predicament then last year at the Grand Canyon of Pennsylvania. Like last year we had to get our bicycles, with our gear aboard, moving from a stopped position, up a steep hill. But this year Sharon and I were further handicapped by our laughter.

Remember Rule #6? As a reminder, Rule #6 is the really stupid one that dictates that we never walk our bikes. It became a matter of pride. No one wanted to be the first to break the rule.

We watched as Shannon and Ouisi made their way slowly up the face of the wall. As tears of laughter ran down our faces, their images slowly faded into the distance.

In time, Sharon and I managed to bicycle up the wall and return to the main route, catching Shannon and Ouisi. We continued to suffer from periodic fits of unexplained hilarity, especially if we happened to catch each other's eye. Shannon and Ouisi were pretty sure we had gone over the edge….but help was near!

The Finger Lakes Region is the oldest wine producing district in the East. The Cayuga Wine Trail is along Routes 79 and 89, one of which we were traveling. After seeing a sign for a winery, Shannon quickly left the road for some wine tasting. No one blamed her. In fact, the rest of us decided that it was a wonderful idea and soon followed her up the slight incline to the winery. The wine was nice, but after a couple of sips I'd had enough. Not Shannon…she needed at least a glass to recover from dealing with our silliness. With around ten miles to go, however, we couldn't dilly-dally any longer.

As day turned into evening, the air cooled to a wonderfully pleasant temperature. We had reached the northern end of Cayuga Lake where the road ran along the shore. Trees lined the road, with the shore just to our right. Aloud, I sighed, "Oh, it is just so pleasant!"

Sharon, biking just behind me, had misunderstood and thought I had said we are almost there. These were the days before any of us had computers for our bicycles that kept track of mileage and speed.

Wondering how I knew how far we still had to go, she asked, "How can you tell?"

Not knowing she had misunderstood my remark, it was beyond me to explain how I knew it was pleasant. The absurdity of the question, combined with being tired from our day's journey, was more than I could take. I was once more overcome with laughter.

A few yards ahead I spotted a park near the lake, and managed to just make it to the grassy area before I tumbled off the bike in hysterics. Sharon followed suit not even knowing why we were laughing. Once again Shannon and Ouisi were clueless as to what had caused this latest fit of laughter. Surely the effects of the ice cream had long since worn off....then again, maybe not. Fortunately, we were close to our destination.

Seneca Falls is at the northern tip of Cayuga Lake. The first settlers arrived in the late 18th century, and the area was known as Mynderse Mills. In April of 1831, the village was renamed Seneca Falls. The first Convention for Women's Rights was held here in 1848, which signaled the birth of the Women's Rights Movement. It has been suggested that Seneca Falls was most likely the inspiration for the fictional village of Bedford Falls in Frank Capra's holiday classic *It's A Wonderful Life*.

We stayed at The Guion House, with proprietor Patricia Dantona, at 32 Cayuga Street, part of the historic District of Seneca Falls. This Second Empire-style home was built by General George M. Guion in 1876. The beautiful, stately mansion still operates as a Bed and Breakfast. Since we had not planned on any evening entertainment, we had a leisurely dinner. Sharon and I thought it best not to order anything that contained ice cream.

July 21st

The next morning I realized we were going to have to consider modifying our route. We had wanted to visit the Rose Hill Mansion before heading south to Burdett, New York, on route 414.

Throughout the years we have made it a point to visit as many old historic homes as we could. All of them are incredible architectural beauties, especially those which have been meticulously preserved. These homes represent an elegance of a distant past that is a significant part of our history and legacy. We have marveled at the attention to detail and the pride of workmanship we see in these homes, qualities that are often lacking in many homes being built today. It has been a privilege to experience our country's past through the tour of these historical sites.

Looking over the map, I saw that we had almost sixty miles to our next destination. Being now particularly sensitive to Rule # 7 (no biking at night), I was concerned that we could not take a tour of the mansion, which was several miles out of our way and still get to our next B&B in Burdett before dark. Until we were properly equipped for night riding, we had to honor rule #7. After a brief discussion, and a reminder of our trip back from the Mark Twain performance, we reluctantly agreed to omit the mansion from the day's schedule.

Off we headed for another day of unknown adventures. We chose to wear our playing card outfits. They were comprised of T-shirts with the different suits displayed in black and red on a white background. The T-shirt was then tastefully complimented by red bandanas and socks.

Our route took us south on 414 along the east side of Seneca Lake, the largest of the Finger Lakes. We had lunch on the way, but did *not* stop for ice cream. Sharon and I had been permanently banned from ice cream for the rest of the trip...hm...we're not really clear as to when this vote was taken. No one has ever said that Shannon and Ouisi aren't wise, their participation on the bike trip notwithstanding.

Not long before we arrived at the Country Gardens Bed and Breakfast, we were stopped by a motorist who asked if he could take our picture. I have no comment.

Burdett is located on the east side of Seneca Lake, just north of Watkins Glen. Route 414 is on a high ridge above the lake, but most of the views of the lake were blocked by forests.

The Country Gardens B&B, hosted by Nancy and Howard Keys, is west of 414. As we turned onto the road to our B&B, we were met by three very fast, vicious dogs that were determined to remove all or part of our legs. All three were large animals that acted as if they had not eaten for a while, and we were their dinner. It had been some time since dogs had chased us, so we had become rather complacent. Being the end of the day, we were also near the end of our physical stamina, or so we thought. Once the dogs hit the road barking and growling, adrenaline poured into our bodies. None of us had any idea we were capable of such speed and power. It goes without saying that we were very impressed with ourselves. In reality, the steep downhill to the B&B was probably what saved us.

Overlooking Seneca Lake, the Country Gardens is a lovely and charming B&B. We were particularly charmed by the gazebo at the far end of the gardens with an uninterrupted view of the lake. We spent most of the evening at the gazebo, enjoying the sunset and recovering from our race with the dogs. We all enjoyed an evening of giggles as we relived our adventures thus far.

Feeling quite the experts on B&Bs, we compiled a list of a few of the most important aspects that a B&B should have for bicycling guests....well, for us anyway.

1. No dogs near the entrance
2. Fabulous breakfast with great coffee
3. Cheery atmosphere and beautiful gardens
4. A three-star or better restaurant nearby that serves beer and wine
5. Must be away from heavy traffic, and preferably not on top of a hill

Once we finished our B&B review, we dealt with the issue all of us had been avoiding. How do we get past the three "bike eaters" blocking our exit? Our B&B was on a dead-end road which was very steep, and we know what that means. Remember the snails. There was no question that these dogs were faster than snails. We were toast...or better described by the dogs as hamburger. We spent the rest of the evening trying to come up with some kind of strategy, knowing that there was a real possibility that the dogs would probably get at least one of us.

"Let us be merry for tomorrow we may die!"

Everything was funny and we laughed until our sides hurt, with tears streaming down our cheeks. Fear will do that. There was no chance that we could outrun the dogs going up a steep hill. We barely outdistanced them on the way in when we had a descent to our advantage. As the evening wore on we were unable to find a solution. The only logical one was that one of us would have to sacrifice herself to save the others. However, we were fresh out of straws.

July 22nd

By morning we were still in a quandary. This was the last day of our trip. To think that we had come so far! Rightly so, we figured our hosts were unlikely to invite us to move in permanently. We consumed our breakfast as if it was our last meal. After stalling for as long as we could, we began our ride up the hill to meet our fate. We went as one with prayers in our hearts. As we neared the location of yesterday's attack, we stayed as close together as possible to present an imposing façade. With fear and trepidation, we came even with the home. Silence!

"With cat-like tread, past the dogs we steal,
In silence dread, our cautious way we feel.
No sound at all! We never speak a word,
A fly's foot fall could be distinctly heard!" (sort-of from *Pirates of Penzance*)

Steadily, we moved passed. More silence....we could barely breathe. God was with us! Apparently, the dogs were still inside. Once we were out of range from a potential dog attack, we collapsed on the side of the road in sheer relief. Thank you! Thank you! Thank you! Our grateful outpouring was followed by songs of joy.

Off we went on a glorious eight-mile downhill ride into Watkins Glen. The town is *so* lovely, nestled in the glacier-formed hills at the southern tip of Seneca Lake. In 1842 the village was incorporated as Jefferson. The name Watkins Glen was adopted in 1852 honoring Samuel Watkins, founder of the community. The area is best known for its role in auto racing. In 1948 Cameron Argetsinger organized the first Watkins Glen Sports Car Grand Prix, marking the revival of American road racing. The U.S. Grand Prix was held in Watkins Glen from 1961-1980. Watkins Glen still hosts many auto races including one of the few races in the NASCAR Sprint Cup Series not conducted on an oval speedway.

Located next to the village is Watkins Glen State Park. In 2005 the park was named as one of Reserve America's "Top Outdoor Locations." Within a two-mile stretch, the Park's stream descends 400 feet past 200-foot cliffs, generating 19 waterfalls. We hiked the gorge path and were mesmerized by the incredible beauty of the four mile hike. Each turn on the trail was another overwhelming feast for the eyes and ears. We spent hours exploring and taking pictures.

Watkins Glen State Park

Having been caught up in the beauty of the Park, time got away from us. Unfortunately, we had to get going. We were to be picked up that afternoon in Corning at the Corning Glass Center, over 20 miles away. It was around eleven when we left the Park. Once again we had made an error. We were leaving Watkins

Glen in the heat of the day.

Our long uphill exit out of Watkins Glen should not have been a surprise. The town is at the southern end of Seneca Lake where the glaciers formed the highest hills as they pushed rock and dirt ahead, creating the deep gorges and ravines. The road up was several miles long, and Sharon now appeared wise since she had the only 21-speed bike. I always wondered why, when we had to ascend these long, difficult mountains, our 30lbs. of gear slowly got heavier. It was my vote that because Sharon was the only one on a technologically advanced bicycle, she should carry our gear. Sharon proved to be a very poor sport about my brilliant suggestion.

With each of us carrying our own gear, and three of us on bicycles not made for long, steep hills, and with the sun beating down on us, we tackled the mountain. The heat was murder on our poor bottoms which were already suffering from four days of bicycling. Mile after mile, with plenty of breaks, we slowly made our way to the top. As with the Olean hill, and all long ascents thereafter, we experienced the same phenomenon of the summit continuing to recede regardless of how much we pedaled. I learned to keep my eyes down and not look up. The one positive on this climb was that we were not passed by any snails. I could choose to interpret this as a gain in our conditioning, but the truth is snails do not travel during the heat of the day. I was beginning to realize that we could learn a lot from snails.

After what seemed like days of biking, but more like a few hours, we made it to the top of the hill, only to collapse in the first grassy area we came to. It is important to point out that, at least in the areas we biked, people do not surround their properties with walls or fences to separate themselves from their neighbors. As I fell to the ground I noticed a home about fifty yards off the road. We lay there in what could be described as a catatonic state. It wasn't long before I heard a door open. The owner of the property was heading our way! Fleeing was not an option, but we were able to sit up. To our complete surprise and delight, the owner, a woman, was carrying a plateful of brownies.

As she approached us she said, "You look like you could use some of these!"

If I had been her, I would have been on the phone to the nearest mortuary to see if I could get someone to come and remove the bodies. However, she could not have been more thoughtful. What a sweetheart! I got the feeling that we were not the first travelers to use her lawn to recuperate on. She probably kept a supply of brownies on hand for just such occasions. Unfortunately, I cannot have chocolate but, not to seem ungrateful, I took one anyway. Once she headed back to her home, I gave it to the others to share. Sharon, not only being a land shark but also a chocoholic to boot, ate most of it.

In our compromised physical state we did not get our benefactor's name, but I added her to our growing list of angels that have been sent to our rescue. After twenty years of biking we now have a rather impressive list. There is no doubt the Lord knows we need all the help we can get.

The trek up the mountain taught us some important lessons:
1. We need a new planner…anyone? Anyone?
2. Learn from snails….do not bike in the heat of the day.
3. Bring plenty of water or PowerAde, supplemented with "Emergen-C".
4. Buy a 21-speed bike.
5. Collapse in a yard where brownies are served.
6. Always be on the lookout for angels…they come in the most surprising forms.

After about 20 minutes of rest, liquids and snacks, we were ready to move on.

It is only fair to point out that in all the grumbling about going up mountains, we do experience a wondrous sense of accomplishment and euphoria when we reach the top. Seeing a daunting task to the end can produce an incredible sense of pride and joy.

Continuing on Route 414, we dropped down into Corning. Realizing our trip was soon to end, I found myself biking slower just to have more time to relish this wonderful experience. Except for my posterior, I was feeling very fit and strong. What a great and fun-filled time! I did not want our trip to end. Tooo much fun!

As we entered Corning, 414 was under construction, being converted into a four lane highway. We always avoid major highways whenever possible. See Rule #1. This time it could not be helped. We took our time as we maneuvered around the traffic and equipment.

Corning is in southern New York near the Chemung River, and is known as the "Crystal City" since it is the home of the internationally known Museum of Glass and the Stueben Glass factory. The city is also the location of the Rockwell Museum which houses one of the East's largest collections of American Western Art, along with the Carder collection of Stueben Glass.

As we waited for our ride back to Glendorn, we toured both the Stueben Glass factory and the Glass Museum. Steuben Glass has been hand-made in Corning since 1903. These incredible pieces are created using a unique optical formula, combined with Steuben's state-of-the-art melting process which insures exceptional purity, free from even the tiniest visible imperfections. All of the engraving is done by hand. There are no "seconds" at Steuben. Our tour included watching the artisans fire the glass and hand engrave the pieces. From there we entered the Museum of Glass, where the self-guided tour began with a trip through the ages, starting with man's first use of glass. Over 20,000 objects are on display. We could have spent hours exploring the museum, but our ride was waiting....so, maybe next year.

**1994**
Approximately 120 miles

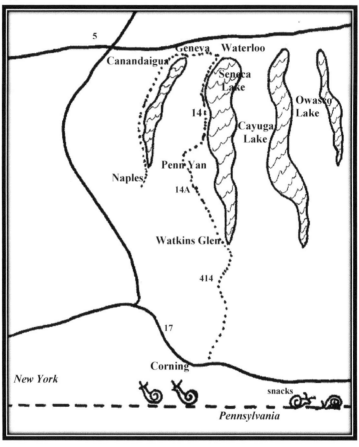

Route ●●●●●●●●

Highways _____

Chapter 5
1994

Pies and Flowers

Life is never stagnant, and for all of us bicycling musketeers, 1993-94 was no exception. Shannon had graduated from college and the last of Ouisi's boys, Blaine and Drew (the twins) along with my oldest son Brad, had graduated from High School. Sharon's daughter, Jean, had just finished elementary school. The year for us mothers and fathers was full of school activities, along with numerous sporting events. Each Saturday, Dick and I had to figure out how we were going to watch all four games. Our youngest son, Garett, was on two different teams. In addition, all of my sons, along with Ouisi's son Drew, were on Odyssey of the Mind teams.

OM is an International problem-solving competition. I coached OM for over sixteen years and it proved to be one of my most rewarding endeavors. The teams gathered at our house to spend hours creating and building their solutions. Dick spent several years on the West Texas OM Board. Our lives seemed to continue to get more hectic, no matter how many New Year's resolutions we made to the contrary.

Regardless of how busy we were, we could not wait to start planning our next biking adventure. After four years of bicycling we had learned a lot, but we had a lot to learn. Finding a new navigator was always a consideration after each trip. Since no one else wanted the job I was not replaced, although once again I was cautioned that I needed to plan easier routes with fewer hills (a.k.a. mountains).

All of us now had 21-speed bikes. We could not let Sharon be the only wimp in the group. After all, there is strength in numbers. Our bikes were all equipped with flashing lights and reflectors. I had a headlight placed on the front of my handlebars, and to keep herself technologically advanced, Sharon purchased a bike computer to keep track of our speed and distances. She had also purchased a bicycle pump. All of us now carried extra bicycle tubes and patch kits.

Our cycling trips do not appeal to serious bicyclists who tear across the countryside over hill and dale trying to see how fast they can travel, not to mention how uncomfortable they can become sleeping outdoors in all kinds of weather. Give us a leisurely pace to see the idyllic countryside and to learn about its history. We take many breaks to photograph its beauty, sample its produce and just bask in its loveliness, all acceptable excuses to rest. We reward ourselves for the many miles we travel by staying in charming and, more importantly, comfortable bed and breakfasts where we are spoiled and fed sumptuous meals (as well we should be).

We enjoy tours of museums and historic mansions along the way and attend local theatres and festivals. What a life! So why were we on these trips for only five days?

July 16st

Year five found us continuing our exploration of the Fingers Lakes region of New York. Our trip started in Naples, New York, which was, not surprisingly, named after Naples, Italy. It is considered the grape pie capital of the world. There are fifteen wineries located within a 20 mile radius of Naples, which is located at the southern end of Canandaigua Lake. Similar to all of the Finger Lakes, Canandaigua Lake is a product of the ice age, which means there are mountains around it.

Pat Wieland, Ouisi's husband, who had been visiting with us at Glendorn, graciously offered to drive us to Naples on his way to the airport. It was only two hundred miles out of his way! Chivalry is not dead! Before he dropped us off at our B&B, we visited the Cumming Nature Center, a 900-acre environmental education preserve located seven miles north of Naples. Since Pat needed to catch a plane, we only took a short hike in this lovely preserve.

Pat left us at the Maxwell Inn, a Greek revival home built around 1841, where the Maxwell family subsequently lived for three generations. After we unpacked, we prepared for our evening out which started with a wonderful meal at the Naples Hotel, known today as the Naples Inn and Suites. Following dinner, we attended the Bristol Valley Theatre where we enjoyed Neil Simon's "Brighton Beach Memoirs."

We'd already had "tooo much fun" and yet we hadn't even been on our bicycles. Bicycles? Are we supposed to bike somewhere? We were so excited to begin our journey the next day that it took a while for us to go to sleep. Our sleep was further postponed by giggles as we reminisced about our past adventures. Maybe we ought to write a book....just a thought.

July 17th

Breakfast consisted of a wonderful selection of fresh fruits and breads followed by eggs, which gave us a perfect start for the day. As it turned out, one of the guests staying at the Maxwell Inn was the star of the previous night's production. We had fun visiting with him letting him know how much we enjoyed the play.

Before leaving Naples, we visited the Hanging Gardens Nursery. Throughout the main part of town we had noticed beautiful hanging containers of flowers displayed on the lampposts. They were gorgeous! After we made a few inquiries, we were directed to the nursery that was responsible for these displays.

As we came through the entrance, we were awe-struck by the grounds which were covered with hanging baskets, displaying a profusion of color.

The nursery had a unique way of planting, using cylinders of various sizes to create the hanging effect. The standard cylinder was made of plastic and was about 18 inches tall. There were four rows of openings in the plastic where seedlings were placed. The opening in the top provides access for watering, or for rain. I ordered several for myself and gave some as Christmas presents. Unfortunately, none of us were able to recreate the spectacular displays we saw in Naples.

Our route on Highway 21 took us north along the west side of Canandaigua Lake, considered by some to be the most beautiful of the Finger Lakes. The lake is 17 miles long and approximately one mile wide. Although we had only a 27 mile jaunt to the town of Canandaigua, we wanted to get there in plenty of time to visit the Sonnenberg Mansion and Gardens.

Canandaigua, from the Seneca Indian name meaning "chosen spot," was the site of the principal village (which John Sullivan later destroyed in 1779) of the Seneca nation. In 1794 the treaty of Canandaigua was signed at this site between the six nations of the Iroquois and United States. The treaty is still recognized today.

With only twenty-seven miles to ride, we did not have many opportunities to get into trouble. Even though we were anxious to get to our bed and breakfast, having chosen the Morgan-Samuels Inn, we did, of course, take our full complement of breaks.

The Inn, listed in the *Select Registry*, is considered by some people to be the crown jewel of the Finger Lakes Wine Country. *Frommer's B&B Guide* named Morgan-Samuels "one of two most beautifully landscaped properties in the seven Mid-Atlantic states." The home sits on a rise surrounded by forty-six acres and is furnished with museum-quality pieces. Breakfast, prepared by the owner, was described as a "memorable, full gourmet candlelit breakfast." The Inn was beyond our budget, but after reading the description, we had to consider it. Gourmet food, elegance, and fabulous gardens were a combination we could not pass up. Heck with the cost! We took a vote…. do we deserve to be treated like royalty? YES! As we biked up the 2000 foot tree-lined drive to The Morgan-Samuels Inn, we knew we had not made a mistake.

Once we had unpacked our bikes we headed over to the 50 acre Sonnenberg Mansion and Gardens State Historic Park. The forty-room Queen Anne-style home was built in 1887. Mary Clark Thompson designed the gardens over a hundred years ago. The nine, themed formal gardens include Italian, Colonial, and Japanese influences. Rose gardens and rock ponds, streams and fountains accent the landscape. What a spectacular wonder! Sharon is a Master Gardener and was completely overwhelmed by the magnitude and variety of each of these gardens.

After we wandered through the park for several hours, it was time for food. It was always time for food. After all, Sharon was on the trip. We had a delightful meal at Casa de Pasta in Canandaigua, accompanied by the now-mandatory beer. What a delightful day! That night we slept like logs.

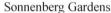

Sonnenberg Gardens

Clayton      Sharon      Ouisi

July 18th

Breakfast the next morning was not a disappointment. The presentation and food were as advertised. Even with over 50 miles ahead of us, we took time to enjoy the beautiful gardens at the Morgan-Samuels Inn. Although we never again stayed at a B&B quite that expensive and luxurious, we had no regrets….we were royalty for a night.

We took Highway 20, crossing from Canandaigua Lake to Seneca Lake, in order to reach the town of Geneva. Being part of the largest wine-producing region in New York, Geneva's major industry is wine making. Geneva also claims to be the "Lake Trout Capital of the World." After riding along the northern end of Seneca Lake, we connected with Highway 5, which took us into Waterloo.

The original celebration of Memorial Day began in Waterloo, New York, in 1865 when a local druggist, Henry Welles, suggested it would be appropriate to remember the dead of the Civil War by placing flowers on their graves. In 1966,

Congress officially recognized Waterloo as the birthplace of Memorial Day.

We were about halfway through our 50 mile day and needed a well-deserved break to grab lunch. Sharon was on the trip. We had lunch at the Crow's Nest where we ordered a gourmet pizza served to us outdoors on the waterfront. After lunch, we backtracked through Geneva then headed south along Seneca Lake on Route 14. Fifty miles was not a bad distance, although we prefer closer to forty. When you add mountains and heat to the mix, fifty miles becomes an entirely different journey.

At this point I probably should mention our training. Training.

The heat certainly was getting to us, so we took more than our usual number of breaks. I had noticed that Sharon was struggling and was often falling behind. I know we had fed her. Since I was the only one who knew where we were going, I thought it important to try to keep us together. Consequently, we made particularly poor time. We had to cross from Seneca Lake to Keuka Lake on Route 54 to reach Penn Yan, our day's destination. Heading west into Penn Yan, there were a few hills to negotiate, which are never welcomed at the end of a day's ride.

Penn Yan was founded by Abraham Waggener in 1833. At the time, half of the inhabitants were Pennsylvanians and half Yankees, hence the name Penn Yan. The term Yankee, as used by the British during the Revolutionary War in referring to the rebel colonists, was "thick with contempt." In 1769 there were a series of clashes over land titles in Pennsylvania in which "Yankee" meant the Connecticut claimants. Since there were equal numbers of Pennsylvanians and Yankees in the town in 1833, the inhabitants recognized both in its name. In 1993, Penn Yan was rated #71 in *The Hundred Best Small Towns in America.*

Having biked the fifty miles, we were done in, especially Sharon. Our bottoms were not very happy either. It was around six o'clock as we entered Penn Yan from the east. We were staying at the Heirloom B&B on the west side of town.

Biking through town, we had come to a stop at an intersection where there happened to be a fire station on one of the corners. At the exact moment we started across the intersection, a city-wide emergency warning was issued from the fire station. The decibels were so loud that we almost fell off our bikes! We had no idea what was going on. I wrongly assumed that the fire station doors were all going to fly open and every truck housed there would be roaring into the intersection, sirens blaring and horns honking.

If we had lived there, we would have known that this was the monthly test of their emergency warning system. It seems to me that they needed a warning system to warn people that there was going to be a test of the warning system…hm.

We had no idea what we were supposed to do. Panic set in! Do we go back, forward, sideways or just fall down in the middle of the street? As the blaring continued we quickly dismounted our bikes and dropped them there in the intersection. It's easy to figure what happened next. True to form, Sharon and I started to laugh and were soon joined by Ouisi. Not being able to stand, the three of us just sat down in the middle of the intersection next to our bikes which had now become a tangled mess.

Shannon had actually made it through the intersection before the emergency test had started. Sharon, Ouisi and I were stuck in the middle of the intersection, suffering from panic, heart seizure, rapid aging, and overcome with laughter. This was not a good combination and certainly not one I would recommend. Fortunately, we were not run over by any of the cars crossing through the intersection. This was important because I could not have handled any additional adversity.

Once the blaring stopped, there was peace and quiet. Dusting ourselves off, we picked up our bicycles, along with several pieces of gear that had come loose, and sheepishly moved out of the intersection. The three of us tried to get back to normal. Well, that was not going to happen. We hoped that the Heirloom Bed and Breakfast was close. NOT. It was several miles further on. We were hot, tired, and were just recovering from experiencing a test of Penn Yan's emergency test system, when we finally reached the turnoff to our B&B. A steep hill blocked our path…again! Ouisi, Sharon and I stopped and watched Shannon slowly pedal up the hill. It was too much…. Rule #6 was null and void…and about time! Without a word, the three of us dismounted and walked up the hill. Sometimes being smart pays off. This demonstration of our mental acuity proved to us that the heart seizure at the intersection had not caused any brain damage…always a welcome confirmation.

We arrived at the Heirloom B&B in a mess. We must have looked awful because our hosts insisted that they drive us to dinner and pick us up afterward. We gladly accepted. I don't think any of us could have bicycled another foot…especially Sharon. She really was not doing well. Her three self-appointed doctors deduced that she was again low on protein and possibly had an iron deficiency. At dinner that night we all strongly encouraged Sharon to order liver, which just happened to be on the menu. After she gave her "doctors" a wilting look, she did as we suggested. I assumed the liver helped since she ultimately finished the trip. This was a perfect example that the end justifies the means. The rest of us felt and looked better than Sharon, a lot better, so we wisely deduced that we could order something else.

It was a fun evening for all and, to add to the festivities, it was our waitress Liz's birthday. By now we were feeling perky, so we all joined in for a rousing rendition of Happy Birthday.

True to their word, our hosts picked us up. You can never be too sure about these things. Considering our state when we arrived, they could have conveniently forgotten about us. If I had been them, I would have definitely considered it.

Before going to bed we took time to evaluate the list of rules that were established five years before. Of course, Sharon still wanted to know "what rules?" With so many years of experience, we should be in a good position to make an informed evaluation. We used the following rating system:

Excellent---great rule....pat ourselves on the back for being so astute
Good---- reasonable and justifiable
Okay----probably not necessary, but doesn't hurt
Stupid----embarrassing to think that we had thought of this rule

Rules evaluation:
1. Avoid riding on interstates or freeways.
   Rating: Excellent...keep rule in force whenever possible. Safety first!

2. Take back roads through scenic and idyllic byways.
   Rating: Excellent....these roads are everywhere and prove to be one of the best parts of each trip.
3. Only ride short, flat mountains...no long, steep ones.
   Rating: Excellent....not realistic, however, unless we plan all of our trips in track and field stadiums. However, staying away from areas with a skier symbol helps.
4. Plan food stops
   Rating: Excellent....according to Sharon, we probably need to plan more of these.
5. Could not be rescued or given a ride anywhere, including going to get something to eat.
   Rating: Stupid....in direct violation of rule #4. These are not just bike trips, they are adventures, and every adventure needs a rescue or two....or ten. What were we thinking?
6. Could not get off our bikes to walk up a steep incline, including mountains.
   Rating: Stupid-no comment necessary.
7. Absolutely no biking at night.
   Rating: Good, but delete "absolutely"....we cannot violate rule #4, so modify the rule to read: "Night biking allowed providing the bicycles have headlights and/or reflectors, with the rider wearing reflective clothing.
8. Must always wear bike helmets.
   Rating: Excellent....needs no justification.

9. Wear coordinated matching outfits.
   Rating: Excellent…..This rule could only have come from a brilliant mastermind.
10. Stay in B&Bs
    Rating: Excellent …this book says it all.

After a thorough discussion, rules #5 and #6 were deleted, while #7 was modified.

Exhausted and with obvious signs of aging caused by our harrowing experience in Penn Yan, all of us applied an extra layer of moisturizer before hitting the sheets.

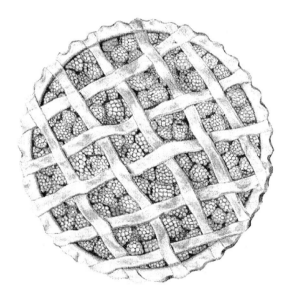

July 19th

Breakfast was wonderful! We ate in their bright, airy sunroom, where we were served French toast stuffed with cream cheese. This was the first time I had tried this dish and I thoroughly enjoyed it.

A wonderful day was ahead of us. We had only 26 miles to Watkins Glen, where we were staying. We headed south on Route 14A through Dundee, connecting with Route 14. Since we had such a short distance to bike, we took our time, stopping often to sample the local produce. As we passed by farms and orchards, we would find wagons laden with baked goods or fruits and vegetables. Each item would be priced, and a box provided in which to place one's money. There was no one around to make sure we paid. We marveled at the genuine sense of honesty and honor. We had a wonderfully delicious time as we grazed from farm to orchard.

At one farm we found a freshly baked raspberry pie that we could not pass up. Securing it to the back of one of the bikes was a challenge. Not only did we have to make sure that it would not fall off, but we also took special care not to crush it. Where there is a raspberry pie, there is a way! We had it for desert that night.

Once again we visited the town of Watkins Glen. The year before, we had stayed east of town on the hillside in Burdett and only had time to visit the State Park as we rode through.

Our B&B, The Seneca Lake Watch was, obviously, on Seneca Lake. We were given an attic room overlooking the shores. Once in our room, we crashed. The heat and several days of bicycling had taken its toll. We all slept for several hours and did not make it to dinner until close to 8:30. We ate at Doug's Wildflower Café, if for no other reason than we loved the name.

July 20th

The next morning we said goodbye to Shannon. She joined some friends who happened to be in the area. I personally believe she had conveniently arranged this to avoid the ride out of Watkins Glen that we had experienced the year before. Of course, she denied it.

Having learned from experience, the three of us left mid-morning to take on the long hill leaving Watkins Glenn. With our twenty-one speed bikes, and riding in a cooler part of the day, we did not suffer the trauma of last year's ascent. At the top we once again took a break on the woman's lawn who had served us brownies, in hopes of being greeted with another plate of goodies. She was nowhere to be seen. Apparently, she saved the treats for the travelers who were closer to death. We must have seemed perkier this year.

Riding on to Corning, we dashed into the glass museum for another visit before being picked up for our return to Glendorn.

As it turned out, this was Shannon's last year to travel with us. She had graduated from college and, after returning to her home town of Denver, she went to work. She always hoped to one day join us for another adventure, but it was not to be. However, I have total confidence that when she reaches her forties she will once again be with us.

**1995**
**Approximately 140 miles**

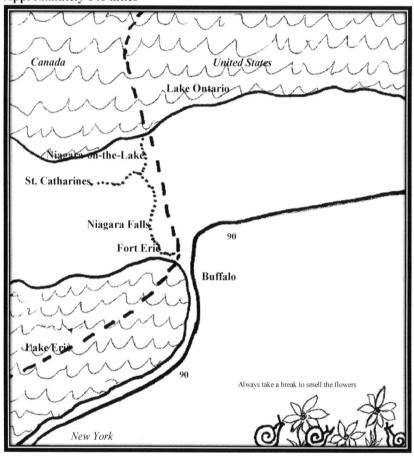

Route ...........

Highway _____

Chapter 6
1995

Forts, Flowers, and Falling Waters

The adult human body resists and protests new physical activities. For example, when we try a new exercise or resurrect an old one, the body warns us, in the form of aches, pains and stiffness, not to try it again. "Stop, or I am going to hurt you!" the body announces. In addition, the body gets worn down when continually challenged with too many physical activities coupled with an improper diet. When we tire, our energy plummets and it is hard to stay motivated, yet many of us are driven to try anyway. Why, one might ask? If you can get past the body's protests and resistance you feel better, can do more, and the body is healthier. There are limits, however, and everyone is different. The younger you start a sport or activity, the less the resistance. Most of us began bicycling at a young age. As the old saying goes, "it is like learning to ride a bike…you never forget."

The remaining three of us, Sharon, Ouisi and I, knew what riding a bike was all about…no problem or protest there. The challenge was to ride farther while negotiating all types of terrain in all kinds of weather, while minimizing aches and pains. Once we started our biking trips, we all experienced a great deal of protest from our bodies. We were warned repeatedly not to bike so far, forget the hills, and be careful of the heat. Shannon, being younger, would probably disagree. We are talking a twenty-year difference in age. This difference might explain why she always had to wait for us. You think?

Over the years we developed a plan that seemed to minimize our body's protests and resistance, but if we misjudged or failed to follow all aspects of our plan, which was by no means perfect, we paid the price. Note that in the list below, training is mentioned last. The three of us have families and a long list of responsibilities that push a consistent training program down on our list of priorities.

The plan, as developed by the fifth year, was as follows:

1. Use up-to-date equipment such as 21 speed bikes. Let the bike do the lion's share of the work…..yeah right!
2. Eat well and enhance fluids by combining PowerAde with Emergen-C to help replace electrolytes lost during our journey….and boy, did we lose electrolytes. The energy used to ride, coupled with the heat and humidity, definitely contributed to our lost electrolytes. Many were lost just getting on and off our bikes! By the time we were able to get our leg over the high bar connecting the seat to the handlebars, while preventing the bike from

falling over as gravity pulled at the weight and dubious balance of our gear, we were exhausted. Electrolytes must have been scattered all around our bikes every time we mounted and dismounted, which we did dozens of times a day. How else do you take a break? Take plenty of trail mix and protein bars for snacks, being sure to stop often to snack… but avoid ice cream.

3. Take less challenging routes….we are still working on this. No matter how hard we tried to avoid hills and mountains, inevitably one or two or six always showed up. Where do they come from?

4. Use medicinal remedies to help the body recover. Let's not forget the beer at the end of the day, which goes a long way to relax tired muscles and sooth the spirit.

5. Training…this is how we sneak in a new activity, by conditioning our bodies before they can mount a protest. This is tricky and must be done with extreme caution. With the three of us in our forties, our bodies put up a lot of resistance to our biking trips. If we trained properly, we experienced only mild aches and stiffness. If we were too aggressive, our bodies would let us know by causing pain or injury, while demanding more rest. It was easy to know when we had over-exerted. We would hobble around looking tired.

My training program, if you can call it that, took a low priority during the nine months of school. Before Glendorn was opened to the public in 1997, I usually arrived a week or two ahead of our planned trip. Glendorn consists of 1000 acres with several miles of roads. Upon arrival, I would assemble my bike and, instead of walking, use it to get around. Along with whoever else was there from the group, I would take a 10 to 20 mile ride each day, either into town or to "ducks crossing" just north of Bradford.

The ride to "ducks crossing" soon became our favorite. It was quiet, with little traffic, and took us out into the country. The name came from a sign near the entrance to a cemetery where we usually "had to take a break." The sign warned motorists to slow down for "ducks crossing." We would bike onto the cemetery grounds and sit by a pond to watch the ducks as they cruised around the water. Can you believe there are actually people who do not like to train? Go figure.

Once Glendorn became public, I no longer had the luxury of training there. Consequently, I spent more time training at home in El Paso. Once the boys were out of school for the summer, I would start riding my bike around the neighborhood. Each week I would add distance without adding time. Before beginning the bike trip, I wanted to be bicycling between ten to fifteen miles a day, four times a week.

Around the sixth or seventh year of our trips, a friend helped me train. He showed me how to do sprints on my bike to build leg muscles and endurance. I really felt the difference in my biking after his help. Even the rest of the group commented on how strong I seemed. That year was probably the high water mark of my physical conditioning.

In 1995 we went international, bicycling entirely in Canada. The year before, Pat and Ouisi had visited Niagara Falls. While in Canada, they had stayed in the charming village of Niagara-On-The-Lake. Several times during last year's trip, Ouisi had raved about the town and the area. It sounded like a bike trip to us!

Niagara-On-The-Lake (NOTL) is located where the Niagara River flows into Lake Ontario in the Canadian Province of Ontario. It is nicknamed "The Loveliest Town in Canada" and was named the "Prettiest Town in Canada" in 1996.

The original village of Onghiara was founded on this site in 1781. During the War of 1812, American forces captured and ultimately destroyed the town. It was later rebuilt by the British and still retains much of its 19th century charm. The many Regency and Classical Revival buildings are considered the best in the country. In fact, the Historic Sites and Monuments Board of Canada has designated part of the center of town as a National Historic District, the only one in Ontario. The Historic District has been considered for nomination as a World Heritage Site. Emphasizing its British heritage, the town features the only Lord Mayor in Canada.

NOTL is the site of historic Fort George which served as headquarters for a division of the British Army during the War of 1812. The Americans captured the Fort during the Battle of Fort George in May, 1813 and used it as a base to invade Upper Canada. However, the Canadians turned the Americans back at the battles of Stoney Creek and Beaver Dams. The British re-took Fort George seven months later. It was restored in the 1930's, and today the fort hosts a number of re-enactments and demonstrations.

I have always had an interest in these old forts and love to visit them. Until now our trips had not allowed for this, and since I am really the only one who professed an interest in forts, exploring them had not been a priority.

NOTL is also home to the Shaw Festival, a summer-long series of theatrical productions featuring the works of George Bernard Shaw and his contemporaries.

July 18th

As we gathered at Glendorn for our trip, we were all struck by how much we were going to miss Shannon. She had been with us from the beginning and, unknowingly, pushed us to go farther and faster. She was the author of the now deleted rule #6. With remarkable foresight I sensed we would become a little lazy without her.

We drove to Buffalo from Glendorn, which is about a two-hour journey, crossed over into Canada, and took the Niagara Parkway north along the Niagara River. As we drove into Niagara-On-The-Lake, we were overwhelmed by the profusion of flowers. They were everywhere, in flower boxes, along the sidewalks and hanging on light posts. The old clock tower, also surrounded by flowers, greeted us as we entered the town.

On the left was the Prince of Wales Grand Hotel, and across the street was the beautifully landscaped Simcoe Park and Sanctuary. Sharon and I were blown away! Of all the many quaint towns and villages we had ridden through, NOTL topped them all.

Unfortunately, we were unable to get reservations in the village for our first night. We did find a B&B outside of town. It turned out to be a typical one story suburban home and the surrounding country was flat and uninteresting. Our hosts, however, were wonderful. We only stayed there one night since we had reservations in town at the Olde Angel Inn for the rest of our trip.

After we arrived at our B&B, we had to reassemble our bicycles. Each year Sharon and I would leave our touring bicycles at Glendorn. We kept our old Fujis at home for training. In order to get our bikes into the car, Sharon and I had to remove some of the parts. On the other hand, Ouisi had hers shipped from El Paso, which required a more extensive breakdown and hence a more complex re-assembly.

Once the bikes were back together, we went for a short workout in order to get a few miles under our belts and, more importantly, to make sure our bikes were in working order. There are always adjustments to be made and there is no telling what might go wrong when we re-assemble them. Don't you just hate having left-over parts? We only did this once a year so, without repetition, re-assembling them was somewhat of a challenge. The most difficult part was fine-tuning the brakes to keep them from rubbing against the rims. I still struggle with this adjustment.

July 19th

The next morning we were all up early in order to move into town as soon as possible. We had a lot to see and did not want to get too late a start on the day's tour. After the bikes were loaded up and we managed to sardine ourselves into the rental car, we headed to NOTL and the Olde Angel Inn.

The Inn is one of oldest operating Inns in North America, dating back to 1815. As we walked in, we were transported back nearly 200 years. The woodwork spoke of centuries gone by. There was a wood paneled pub to the left and a charming restaurant to the right. As always, our rooms were upstairs. Sharon and I shared an adjoining bath with Ouisi. The floors were made of 12 to 14 inch wide solid wood planks which showed their history. To think of what those floors had experienced! The ghosts of elegantly dressed men and women, claimed to be seen even today, lend further credence to the many haunting stories that are told of the Inn.

Everything was just too exciting! If it had not been for Ouisi's excitement over her visit from the year before, we probably would not have gone to NOTL. Thank you, Ouisi!

In addition to being in a foreign country for the first time on our bike tours, we had changed our biking routine. In the past, we would start from one location, bike to another each day, and be picked up at the end of the journey. This meant that we had to take all of our gear with us each day. Not only did the gear add weight to our bikes, but we were always having to adjust the bungeed packs in order to prevent the bicycles from falling over, which they did on a regular basis. Our bungeed stack behind our seat had continued to gain in height and instability. Since we biked out from the Olde Angel Inn each day and returned each night, all of our gear could be left in our rooms. We only took a tool bag, a tire pump, and of course, snacks.

For our first day we headed west to St. Catherines along the shores of Lake Ontario. The bikes felt so light and, with the flat countryside, we just flew down the country lanes surrounded by open fields and acres of grapevines. At the time of our visit, the area around NOTL and St. Catherines had only a few vineyards and wineries. Today there are dozens.

St. Catherines was built on the shores of Lake Ontario. Often referred to as St. Kitts, it is the largest city in the Niagara Region and, as of 2006, had a population of 131,989. It is at St. Kitts that the northern end of the Welland Canal begins.

The rivers and lakes of the region were for decades the primary mode of transportation, but the Niagara River, with its impassable falls, blocked entrance to Lake Erie. After many years of debate as to where and how, the Welland Canal was constructed to provide a passage from Lake Ontario to Lake Erie, bypassing Niagara Falls. Because there is a 326 ft. difference in the water levels between the lakes, it was necessary to construct locks to allow boats to travel between the two lakes. The first Welland Canal, finished in 1828, was 28 miles long, with forty locks. Eventually the number of locks was reduced to twenty seven.

Before heading into St. Kitts we visited one of the Welland Canal locks. As we arrived a ship was just entering the lock. I had never witnessed a lock in action, and the technology was fascinating. Locks provide a method for boats to travel between bodies of water of different heights. As the boat goes through the lock the water level is either raised or lowered depending on which direction the boat is headed. Large doors front and back lock the boat in while the water level is

Canal Lock

adjusted. Once the water height matches the exit level, the boat is released. Several locks are often required in order to bring the boat to the required water level. Although the process took some time, we all wanted to stay until the ship was released.

Once again time was working against us. Due to our move into town we had a very late start leaving Niagara-On-The-Lake. Since the procedure of moving a boat through a lock takes a great deal of time, it was already mid-afternoon before the boat was released. As easy as our ride had been, it was too late in the day to continue on to St. Kitts. Reluctantly, we headed back to NOTL knowing we would miss the 1000 acres of groomed parks, gardens and trails that gave the city the official nickname "The Garden City."

Once we were back at the Inn we took our time getting ready for our evening out. We had a lovely dinner at the restaurant in the Olde Angel Inn, followed by a leisurely stroll along Main Street. Later, as I snuggled under the covers, I thought I heard footsteps and whispered voices of lovers long since departed. I am sure I imagined it…or did I?

July 20th

Knowing the meaning of different terms is important for almost any endeavor. Planning bicycle trips is no exception. In choosing a place to stay, the term bed and breakfast means bed and breakfast are provided for the given rate. An Inn is a place to stay and, although they may have a restaurant, meals are not normally included in the rates. Not only was breakfast not included, the Olde Angel Inn's restaurant did not open until lunch. So, early the next morning the three of us walked the block to Main Street in search of a place to get something to eat. We soon found a great breakfast place, the Buttery. The restaurant offered many fabulous dishes to choose from, including eggs Benedict and all kinds of fresh breads.

After breakfast we headed back to the Inn to get ready for the day's trip. We planned to bike south to Niagara Falls. From NOTL there is a bike/walking path that runs south overlooking the Niagara River while paralleling the Niagara Parkway. The paved path begins at Fort George and takes you near the outskirts of the city of Niagara. This was our first ride on a biking trail, and the path could not have been more delightful as it weaved among the trees and shrubs along the cliff overlooking the turbulent Niagara River. Now this was the way to bicycle...no gear to haul, no cars, a relatively flat paved surface and spectaculars views! We could have gone forever. It was, however, only about 14 miles to the end of the bike trail. Rats!

The trail took us through Queenston Heights, the site of several critical battles in Britain's defense of Upper Canada during the war of 1812. Part of the main street is lined with incredible rock walls that remain much as they were when constructed centuries ago. Thin rocks, about three inches thick, were stacked on

top of each other without the aid of concrete. We were very impressed with the craftsmanship. To add to our delight, flowers were everywhere.

As we entered Niagara and our secluded path ended, the traffic became overwhelming. We were not at all happy about trying to negotiate through the multitude of cars on our way to the falls. It was just too dangerous and none of us had the lightning-quick reactions needed to avoid the rushing autos. It did not take long before the screeching brakes and honking horns got to me. Unanimously, we decided to forego the falls and return to Niagara-On-The-Lake.

Since it was on our way home we stopped to visit the Niagara Park Botanical Gardens, also home of the Butterfly Conservatory. The entrance to the Park is on the Niagara Parkway just north of the falls. The 99 acre garden was established in 1936, and is beautifully maintained. It includes a large number of perennials, rhododendrons and azaleas, along with a formal parterre garden with shade, herb and vegetable plantings. The grounds also house an aviary, and the world-famous rose garden which has over 2400 roses. We walked along footpaths which took us past the butterfly garden, the ponds, and an arboretum featuring one of Canada's finest collections of ornamental trees and shrubs.

Most people go to Niagara Falls to see the falls, which are spectacular. But the Botanical Gardens are a wonderful sanctuary to escape the hustle and bustle of hundreds of tourists.

Our return trip to NOTL was just as delightful as our trip to Niagara. We welcomed the peace and quiet of the bike path, while seeing the countryside from a different direction. If we eliminate the short period of congested traffic, our second day in Canada was close to perfect.

That night we went to the theatre. We had purchased tickets to "You Never Can Tell," a play by George Bernard Shaw. With a population of only 15,000, it is impressive that NOTL has three theatres, all of which are used for the annual Shaw Festival. The productions attract incredible talent from all over, and the shows are usually booked weeks, if not months, in advance. We had made our bookings in April.

The three of us had such fun! We dressed for the occasion and, before going to the theater, we stopped at the Prince of Wales Grand Hotel for cocktails and hor'deurves. This beautiful hotel is pure elegance, with the proper Victorian English decor. We had champagne with pate de foie gras in the Queen's Royal Lounge. Were we uptown or what? Upon leaving the hotel we joined the dozens of theater-goers as we made our way to the performance. There was such an air of excitement!

Once in the theater, we were shown to our seats. As I sat there waiting for the curtain to rise I found it hard to believe that we were at a theater in Canada, on a bicycle trip. How truly incredible! After a delightful performance we conformed to after-theater etiquette and had a light supper. Before going back to our B&B we strolled along Main Street, enjoying a splendid midsummer's eve. I don't think any of us wanted the day to end.

July 21st

We still wanted to visit Niagara Falls and certainly could not leave the area without seeing them. This just isn't done and could possibly create an international incident, but we weren't excited about trying to negotiate the heavy tourist traffic around the falls. It was estimated that around 20 million tourists visited the falls in 2008.

The name Niagara is said to come from the Iroquois word "Onguiaahra" meaning "thunder of waters." The original inhabitants were the Iroquois tribe of Ongiara.

The falls were formed during the last ice age, about 10,000 years ago. When the glaciers receded, they bulldozed a path through the Niagara Escarpment leaving behind the Great Lakes. The interaction of three major rock formations in the Niagara River caused uneven erosion. The underneath was comprised of a soft layer that over time undercut the hard cap rock, which eventually caved in, carving out the falls. When the falls were first formed they were several miles downstream near present-day Queenston. The on-going undercutting continues to move the falls southward. The jumble of rocks seen at the present day location was the result of a giant rock slide in 1954, continuing the fall's retreat.

"Although engineering has slowed erosion and recession in this century, the falls will eventually recede far enough to drain most of Lake Erie, the bottom of which is higher than the bottom of the falls."[1]

Because the Niagara River straddles the international border between Canada and the United States, part of the falls are on each side. The American and Bridal Veil Falls are on the American side, while the more famous Horseshoe Falls is on the Canadian side. Horseshoe Falls drops about 173 feet and is 2600 feet wide.

Niagara Falls is the most powerful waterfall in North America and is valued not only for its beauty, but also as a source of hydroelectric power. Maintaining the balance between recreational, commercial, and industrial uses has been a challenge for the stewards of the falls since the 1800's.

Determined to visit the falls, we decided to put our bikes in the rental car and drive the full length of the Niagara Parkway, which runs from Fort George at NOTL south to Fort Erie. From Fort Erie, we biked back to the falls along the Parkway. It was about twenty miles to the overlook. This proved to be a brilliant

[1] Niagara Falls Wikipedia encyclopedia

solution because the traffic was light, and we biked along sidewalks through residential areas where overhanging trees helped keep us cool. The approach brought us to the overlook from the south along the Niagara River above the falls.

After reaching the falls, we locked up our bikes and joined the hundreds of people at the overlook where, during the peak runoff, over 202,000 cubic feet of water per second flows past and over the drop-off. The falls have to be seen and heard to appreciate the sheer volume of water that flows past, and the crescendo it creates. There are no words that can describe the effect this has on visitors.

On the way to Horseshoe Falls

Clayton          Ouisi

There is something in our human makeup that draws us to moving water. We seem to be mesmerized by it and can watch indefinitely as it constantly changes. Most likely, there have been numerous studies done to try to explain this phenomenon. I was thrilled just to have the opportunity to enjoy the experience.

There is a perpetual whirlpool about a half mile below the falls where the

Niagara River bends to the left. After we had lunch near the whirlpool overlook, we headed back to our bicycles.

Our return trip to Fort Erie was accomplished at a leisurely pace. Since we arrived mid-afternoon, we had plenty of time to explore the fort for which the town was named. Although this was not Sharon's and Ouisi's first choice, they were good sports and agreed to see the fort with me.

Fort Erie was constructed in 1764 and was used as a supply depot for British troops during the American Revolution. During the War of 1812 the Americans captured it, as they did Fort George. After destroying it in 1814 the Americans returned to Buffalo. It was not until the 1930's that the fort was rebuilt. Each August, the 1814 battle, The Siege of Fort Erie, is re-enacted. This was the bloodiest battle fought on Canadian soil.

Once we finished the tour of the fort, we loaded up our bicycles and drove back to NOTL. That evening we enjoyed a nice dinner in the pub at the Olde Angel Inn. They offered a scrumptious Guinness oyster stew that was to die for. The next day was to be the last day of our trip. None of us were looking forward to leaving.

July 22nd

Since we were flying out of Buffalo that afternoon, we decided we had enough time to ride the bike trail one last time. We took off early so we wouldn't have to hurry. On our first trip along the path we had noticed a small chapel set in an opening across the Parkway. We had so much to be thankful for that it seemed appropriate for us to stop and give thanks.

All too soon, it was time to head back. We still had to finish packing and get our bikes ready for the trip. After the car was loaded, we took one more stroll down Main Street to visit some of our favorite shops and take in the lovely atmosphere of this charming village.

Years later, I was to return to Niagara-On-The-Lake, but not for any reason that I could have foreseen at the time.

**1996**
Approximately 155 miles

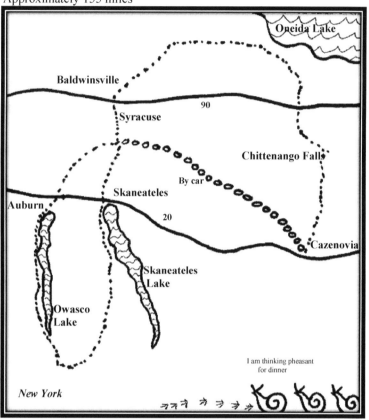

Route     •••••••••••••

Highway    _____

By car    **OOOOOOOOO**

Chapter 7
1996

It was a Very Pheasant Day

Our annual bike trip was almost canceled in 1996. My husband of 26 years passed away that year. Two months after we were married in 1970, he lost his kidneys to glomerulonephritis. Dialysis and transplantation were still in their infant stages of development. Dick was a stubborn and courageous man who fought to the end. He underwent over 35 surgeries, including four kidney transplants. His tolerance for pain became legendary. Although he was restricted by numerous hookups, within hours after surgery, regardless of the pain, he would force himself to get out of bed and walk. Soon after being freed from the monitors and tubes he would walk down all twelve flights of stairs at the hospital and back up every night. There was little question that his determination extended his life. In addition to wanting to see the youngest of our three boys graduate from high school in 2000, Dick was determined to be around for the new century. Although he was able to push his body and make it through one crisis after another, the years of trauma finally took their toll. He died July 1, 1996, leaving an incredible legacy of which our sons and I are tremendously proud.

We are all so fortunate to have our health and the opportunity to do something with our lives. Dick's life and his fight demonstrated how all of us can overcome adversity and still accomplish so much with whatever time we are given. He was tremendously talented. Not only did he have an incredible IQ, but also as a freshman in high school he was selected first chair clarinet to the Texas All-State Band, and in his junior and senior year played varsity football.

Within the first five years of his illness both femoral arteries were ligated due to transplant complications. Without a normal arterial supply of blood to his legs it was difficult for him to walk, let alone run or workout. His mental sharpness was impaired as he suffered chronic anemia. He never complained about how unfair it was and, more importantly, he never used his illness as an excuse for not trying or as a cause for any failure. After he lost his kidneys he received a Masters degree in Engineering and a Bachelor's degree in Business from the University of Texas at Austin. He owned his own management company and still had time to serve on several boards, along with being the baseball commissioner for the boys Little League in El Paso, Texas.

Because of Dick's death, I just could not think about our bike trip. We were to leave July 14, which was only two weeks after his passing and, coincidently, his birthday. Sharon and Ouisi took matters into their own hands and changed the dates. I really had no choice. "We are going," they emphatically told me.

Earlier in the year Ouisi had told us that she was not sure she could go on the bike trip, but Dick's passing changed her plans. I know she did this for me and I was so grateful, for our trip was just what I needed. When Dick died I felt like hiding in a corner, without energy to deal with anything…. "please let the world go away and leave me alone!" However, I had three boys to think of and Dick's business to run. With so little strength and so much pain, I was overwhelmed. I was truly blessed by my sister and dear friend who knew just what to do.

August 27th

Our sixth year brought us back to the Finger Lakes region of New York. We flew into Buffalo, rented a car and drove to Glendorn to pick up our bikes. Instead of taking her bicycle on the plane, Ouisi had her bike shipped to Glendorn. From there we headed east along New York 86, and then connected with 390 north. We picked up Interstate 90 east and headed towards Syracuse. From 90 we dropped down to Auburn, located at the north end of Owasco Lake.

The first settlers moved into the area in 1793. The name Auburn came from a locale mentioned in Oliver Goldsmith's poem "Deserted Village." With the opening of the state prison in 1817 and the establishment of a theological seminary in 1829, Auburn experienced significant growth. The Fort Hill cemetery in Auburn contains the graves of William Seward, secretary of state under Presidents Lincoln and Johnson, and of Logan, a Mingo Indian orator. Auburn was also the home of abolitionist Harriet Tubman.

We had booked rooms for the first and last night of our tour at the Springside Inn, which has been featured in *Country Inns and Back Roads.* Springside was opened in 1851 as a boys boarding school by the Reverend Samuel Robbins Brown who later became the first missionary to Japan.

Over the years Springside has been owned by several different families. During our stay, the Inn was owned by Bill Dove, a second generation member of the Miller family who bought Springside in 1941.

The Inn is large and has grounds extending to a nearby lake. The property has been maintained beautifully, with considerable effort made to uphold its historical authenticity. Springside Inn has its own restaurant and we thoroughly enjoyed our dinner there. That evening we explored the Inn and found a large, delightful room probably used for their dinner theater and banquet hall. Also to our delight, we found an old jukebox that still worked. We selected some great oldies from the sixties. Once the music started, we became dancing maniacs.

Sharon and I, as well as many members of our family, have always loved dancing. We have spent many an evening at Glendorn dancing into the early hours of the morning. Dancing has always been a great way for me to just "let it all go."

The more I danced the better I felt. I have heard from many athletes that part of what drives them is the endorphin euphoria that comes from exercise. Without a doubt the three of us released many endorphins that night at Springside. For the first time since Dick's death I felt the tension and sadness start to fade.

After flying around the dance floor for a couple of hours we headed outside to enjoy the cool evening. At the lake's edge we sat on the dock watching a faint mist slowly move across the water. Except for a slight lapping of water against the shore, there wasn't a sound. We spoke in whispers.

August 28th

The next day we left for Baldwinsville, northwest of Syracuse. From Auburn we biked north on Route 34, crossed Interstate 90 where we picked up Route 370 which took us into Baldwinsville. Our route was over thirty miles long and took us past many farms and bucolic pastures.

The area was settled by John McHarrie, but was named after Dr. Jonas Baldwin who settled there to start the community in 1808. The town is located on the old Erie Canal which is now part of the New York State Barge Canal system.

Grace Episcopal Church of Baldwinsville was one of the first churches in the United States to use electric lighting. For decades the town's economy was fueled by agriculture and industry but, as they declined, Baldwinsville evolved into an attractive and picturesque community. We stayed at Pandora's Getaway, a handsomely restored Greek Revival home constructed in 1845. The home is listed on the National Register of Historic Places.

August 29th

Our hosts, Sandy and Harold Wheeler, served our breakfast the next morning. With few exceptions, the wonderful and beautifully prepared morning meals at the numerous B&Bs we have stayed at were a perfect start to our day of bicycling. Not only have we enjoyed lovely, nutritious meals provided by our hosts, but they also have been a great source of information about the area. We have been given suggestions of what to see, along with some critical information as to the best routes and, more importantly, what ones to avoid.

From Baldwinsville we biked east toward Oneida Lake and then turned south on Route 13 toward Cazenovia. After we biked through the village of Chittenango, we started up a steep mountain on our way to Chittenango Falls State Park. As we slowly biked up the steep incline, I realized that it had been two years since we had biked up a mountain, the last being at Watkins Glen. How quickly I had forgotten how tough it was to ascend a steep mountain on a bicycle! We were going so slow it was amazing that we didn't fall over. Once again the snails had long since passed us in their haste to get out of the way before we fell on top of them. The last curve up the mountain was a killer. Once we reached the summit and the park entrance, we had to take a break. Sharon quickly looked around for someone with brownies...well...one can always hope.

Since we needed some rest we took our time walking around the park, viewing Chittenango Falls and hiking on one of the trails. It was important to convince our leg muscles that they would be used for activities other then the cruel and unusual punishment of biking up steep mountains.

Chittenango Falls cascades 167 feet over a forty million year old bedrock. The park offers fishing and nature trails for hiking. Most importantly, it is the home to the endangered Chittenango Ovate Amber Snail. Live specimens of the Chittenango snail cannot be found anywhere else on earth. No wonder the snails were scurrying out of our way as we biked up the mountain!

After an extended R&R, we treated our leg muscles to a relaxing downhill ride which took us into the village of Cazenovia, located on the southern end of Cazenovia Lake. John Lincklaen, who built the Lorenzo mansion at the south end of the lake, founded the town in 1793. The village is on a hill which overlooks the lake. Albany Street, the main thoroughfare with delightful shops and restaurants lining the street, retains its historic architecture.

We stayed at the Brewster Inn which also sits at the southern tip of Cazenovia Lake. It was built in 1890 as a summer home by financier Benjamin B. Brewster. Brewster, along with John D. Rockefeller, started the Standard Oil Co. The interior of the Inn is exquisitely decorated with mahogany and antique quartered oak.

Entering the grand foyer, we felt and looked bedraggled. The cats had to drag us in! At that moment our host, Dick Hubbard, was just finishing checking in a guest. Another guest passed by while we waited. Seeing the other guest, Dick called to him by name, informing him that his order was ready in the bar. With seventeen rooms, a restaurant and bar, the Inn was more a hotel then a B&B. I was very impressed not only with the attention Dick paid to his guest's needs, but also that he was able to call him by name.

While we were checking in Dick asked where we had been biking and our plans for the next day. As navigator, I told him we were heading back to Auburn by way of Route 20. He quickly warned us that Route 20 between Cazenovia and Skaneateles was one steep hill after another with very little shoulder. Many big 18-wheelers use 20 to cross the state. Even bicyclists from Colorado were more than challenged by the terrain and traffic. It was obvious that he was very concerned.

We shared a few of our biking adventures with him, in particular our trek up the mountain out of Watkins Glen and how grateful we were to be treated to brownies at the top. In the course of the conversation, it was mentioned that I was not able to enjoy the gesture, because I do not eat chocolate.

Dick was a very engaging host and wonderful to tease and have fun with. He fit right in with our group, laughing at the stories and adventures we shared with him. In turn, we learned how he and his wife had purchased the property and renovated it. There is no question he loves what he does and truly cares about his guests.

Our rooms were in the newly-remodeled carriage house. After we cleaned up, we took Dick's advice and had dinner at the Inn. There were several lovely restaurants nearby but having one so close won the day. Soon after we were seated, Dick entered the dining room and made the rounds, welcoming everyone by name. At this point in the evening we were so tired that we became very silly in recounting our adventures. What a surprise! This was one of the first times I had really laughed after losing my husband and it felt wonderful. Laughter really is "the best medicine."

Next to our table was a woman that kept repeating the same comment with every sentence. Unfortunately, neither Sharon nor I have been able to remember the comment. Whatever it was, it became predictable and therefore very comical. Every time she spoke, we knew what was coming. The more we tried not to laugh, the harder we laughed until we were in danger of sliding off our chairs. As soon as we would gain control of ourselves she would make the same comment again and we would once again wilt with laughter.

I cannot imagine what the other patrons thought. Although we didn't really make much noise, we did exhibit our usual physical manifestations of mirth. As is normal, I stopped breathing and just shook while Sharon pounded her feet and hands. Ouisi was more polite and well mannered, but even she was losing control. Our biggest challenge was timing our food and drink intake in order not to be in the middle of a swallow or bite when our neighbor repeated her incessant phrase. We weren't always successful, which made matters worse. Obviously, we thoroughly enjoyed our meal which, when we were able to eat it, was delectable.

When we returned to our rooms we discussed whether or not to stick to our original plan to bike back to Auburn via Route 20. It was twenty-four miles from Cazenovia to Skaneateles. As the past had taught us, changing our route always caused trouble. Besides, I was not able to find an alternate route because the other roads to the south had little skiers on them. We knew what that meant, and to the north was Syracuse, which is a large city and one to avoid. With that in mind we decided that we would go for it. How bad could it really be?

As we readied for bed we once again relived our evening by mimicking the lady next to us who had caused so much hilarity, which then brought on another bout of laughter. Exhausted, we slept like doornails.

August 30th

While getting ready for breakfast the next morning, an alarm went off…a very loud alarm. None of us smelled smoke or saw any cause for concern. When I peeked out the door and into the hall, there wasn't a stampede of guests rushing for the exit. In fact, there was no one in the hall. The alarm continued blaring so we had to assume that something was wrong. It was a little disappointing that no one rushed to our rescue. After all, we could have been overcome by smoke and lying unconscious on the floor of our room.

Immediately after we entered the main house, we rushed over to tell Dick that the alarm at the carriage house was going full blast and, even though we did not need to be rescued, other guests might need his attention. We then went calmly into breakfast.

Before we were finished with our meal, Dick came in to report all was well. He also said that during the night he had decided that Route 20 was really too dangerous and had come up with a solution. His chef was getting married that day, and since he was heading in our direction anyway, he insisted on giving us a ride past the roller coaster of hills. He had already arranged to take our bikes and us in his van, so all was settled.

His knightly armor was further polished to a perfect shine when he presented us with a plate of peanut butter cookies he had baked the night before. He informed us that he was not going be out-done by some little old lady with brownies.

Although so many of our hosts have been wonderful, we have had only two that have qualified for full knighthood. However, because the other knight never could find his polish, his armor was never very shiny. But that's another story.

Since Dick did not drive us on Route 20 to our drop-off point, we did not see what we had been spared. There has always been a part of us that felt we could have biked that section. Although we were slow, we were tough, or so we thought. After all, we were seasoned bicyclists….right? Actually, we were more than likely merely suffering from delusions of grandeur.

Years later Sharon and I drove that section of Route 20 just to see what Dick was so concerned about and to see if we thought we could have risen to the challenge. After we drove it we decided we could have biked the hills. However, there would have been no way to avoid being flattened by the speeding trucks. Once again we had been saved from a dangerous situation by the timely intervention of an angel in disguise.

I have returned to the Brewster Inn two or three times, not only to thank Dick, but also to see how he was doing, only to find him gone. On several occasions Sharon had tried to reach him by phone, but without success.

Once we were dropped off and said our goodbyes, the three of us headed south to Skaneateles. The road, which did not have much of a shoulder, took us through farmland and pastures. We stopped often to take pictures of the many wonderful barns, all of them unique in their own way and in various states of repair. Being the end of August, the corn fields were mature, with stalks loaded with corn.

As I led us through the pastoral countryside, with cornfields crowding the road, a pheasant shot out from among the corn stalks just as I passed. His path to the other side of the road was blocked by me. The pheasant was totally unprepared for my presence, especially me being on a bicycle. I judged by his expression that this was his first bicycle encounter. He took one frantic look up, turned in the same direction I was biking, and ran along next to my foot. Not knowing what else to do, I kept pedaling. The pheasant kept running as fast as his legs would take him, only to look up every few steps with big confused eyes to find that he had not made any progress in getting around the obstacle. He would then lower his head and, with renewed determination, run further up the road to try to outdistance me. This was probably the only race in history between a pheasant and a bicyclist. His frantic expressions started me laughing. So there we were, me trying to stay on the bike while laughing and looking down at the pheasant, while he ran alongside looking up at me, thoroughly undone by the fact I was still there.

In the meantime, Sharon and Ouisi were witnessing this whole turn of events. They found the entire scene extremely entertaining. In hysterics, they had even a harder time keeping control of their bicycles as they watched the contest

between the pheasant and me. Although I had a closer view of the hapless bird as it ran beside my pedal, they were able to witness the entire exchange between us. According to Sharon, we both looked a little frantic as we continued eyeing each other.

Sharon saw this event as an opportunity to secure pheasant for dinner as she licked her chops and mentally sharpened her knife in preparation for the upcoming feast. Ouisi, who was behind Sharon, had a limited view but was able to tell that there was some large bird running next to me. Being less mercenary then Sharon, she did not look on this confused pheasant as dinner. However, Ouisi would not have turned down a pheasant dinner if, perchance, it did not survive the ordeal by either getting tangled in the bike or suffering a heart seizure which, from my point of view, was the most likely outcome.

As the four of us, Sharon, Ouisi, the pheasant and I, continued down the road, I sensed a change in my new best buddy, the pheasant. At this point the poor bird seemed to forget why he was trying so hard to get across the road but, whatever the reason, it was not worth tangling with me. I imagine its primary concern was that the whirling monster next to him was planning to have him for dinner. The pheasant was wrong about the bicycle but, unbeknownst to him, Sharon was closing fast, dinner napkin in place. Our feathered friend, not nearly as dumb as his expression had indicated, reconsidered and decided not to cross the road. Turning on a dime, he bolted back into the cornfield.

There was, of course, no way we could continue biking. We had to take a break. With all that the pheasant and I had been through, I half expected him to rejoin me on the side of the road in order to recuperate and relive the event. Even if that had been a consideration, the appearance of two more bicyclists would have been too much for him.

It was some time before we were able to get back on our bicycles. Each of us took turns telling the story from her point of view. In looking back on the event, I am a little surprised that at least one motorist did not stop to render aid. All three bicycles lay on the ground while we convulsed with laughter next to them. I suppose, without us being aware, we were foaming at the mouth and anyone passing by did not want to get involved with rabid bicyclists…very dangerous.

Once back on our bikes, it was not long before one of us would start thinking of the pheasant and begin laughing again, which only set off the other two. We were off our bikes again, choking with laughter as we lay in the dirt. Our progress was even slower than usual. Tooo much fun!

Over the years the tale about the pheasant has been one of the more requested stories as we recount to friends and family our many misadventures. To this day I cannot pass a cornfield without thinking of our pheasant. This story is a particular favorite of Sharon's daughter, Jean. As a teenager, Jean often asked her mother to tell the story. One evening, with a few friends over, Jean yelled out to her Mom to please tell her friends the "peasant story." From that point on we always refer to this event as the "peasant story," making it even more fun in the telling.

We stopped in Skaneateles for a picnic lunch at Clift Park on the shore of Skaneateles Lake. The town has a full calendar of summer events such as the Antique and Classic Boat Show, hot air balloon rides, polo matches, music in the Park and much more. During the winter months the lake offers ice fishing and skating, while the surrounding hills are perfect for sledding and skiing. Skaneateles is an Iroquois word meaning "long lake." The historic downtown district dates back to 1796.

Stress Free Zone---NOT according to our friend the pheasant.

After lunch we headed down the west side of Skaneateles Lake where we connected with Route 38 in order to reach the west side of Owasco Lake. From there we headed north to Auburn. After reaching the summit of the ridge bordering the west side of Owasco Lake,...yes...we had to take a break. This time the three of us sat next to each other with our backs to the road on a rather wide dirt expanse. As we munched peanut butter cookies, we all decided that, from the motorists' point of view, we looked like the "hear-no-evil, see-no-evil, and speak-no-evil" monkeys. That vision caused us to start laughing again, but in a more subdued manner....we just sat there shaking.

Sitting there between my sister and close friend, looking out over this phenomenal vista, I knew the worst of my grieving was behind me. I had needed to reach this moment before I could heal enough to go on with my life. That isn't to say that there would not be bad times ahead, but my heart and soul were lighter and stronger. God had given me strength and healing. I knew then with absolute certainty that on returning home I could be both Mom and Dad to our sons, while running Dick's business.

With only a few miles to go before we reached the Springside Inn, Ouisi took the lead for the first time in all the years we had been biking together. Sharon and I just looked at each other. I remembered wondering what it meant. Subconsciously I think we all knew that this would be her last trip.

Oh, but the memories of the roads we had traveled together, the people we had met, and all the animals, from dogs to bears (and of course the snails), we had seen…those that crossed our path, or those that tried to, and those that passed us! Even though on the way up a mountain the going is tough, you have the thrilling, incredible ride down. For every uphill we faced we found the downhill, and on the top of some of the toughest mountains there were brownies and peanut butter cookies.

On the roads

**1997**
**Approximately 180 miles**

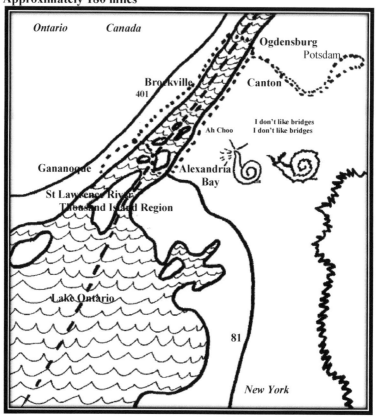

Route     ••••••••••••

Highway     _____

Chapter 8
1997

The Trouble with Goldenrod

As we had foreseen, 1996 was Ouisi's last trip with us. With all of their boys in college, Ouisi and Pat spent more time traveling together. Now there were only Sharon and I.

My two oldest boys, Brad and Colter, were away at college. In the autumn of 1996, before Colter left for his freshman year at Colorado State University, he sincerely offered to postpone college for a year in order to stay in El Paso to help me with Dick's property management business. It was tempting to take him up on his offer, but I knew he needed to go to school and I had to think of what was best for him. Dick had worked so hard in order for the boys to attend college. I knew he would be disappointed in me if I had not insisted that Colter get started on his degree.

1996-1997 was a challenging year and quite a learning experience for me. By the first anniversary of Dick's death, with God's help and encouragement from family and friends, I was amazed by what I had been able to accomplish. At first as I tried to handle the business, learn basic computer skills and juggle everything else, I clearly had earned an F minus. There were days I just closed the door to my office and cried. But too many people were counting on me, including myself. I was not going to quit. So, slowly and after many mistakes, I learned. To add insult to misery, I turned fifty.

Garett, my youngest son, and I were the only ones left at home. By the summer of 1997 he had completed his freshman year in high school.

All three of the boys are very intelligent and athletic. Garett was enrolled in several advanced courses while playing football, wrestling and running track. I left work each day in time to make every game or competition as well as most of his practices. It was my favorite time of day.

Sharon had now been a single mom for nine years and had been working at a preschool. The position was perfect since her working hours were the same as her daughter Jean's school hours. The best part was that she had summers off. Jean was thirteen and officially a teenager with all the drama that girls have during those early developmental years.

Even though the musketeers were down to two, Sharon and I were eager to continue our trips. We decided to head north to the St. Lawrence River and the Thousand Island Region.

August 20th

In time it was bound to happen. The best laid plans of mice and bicyclists are sometimes sabotaged. The night before Sharon and I were to leave for our bicycling trip, our host, Robert Bach, from Bach's Alexandria Bay Inn, telephoned to inform us that our bicycles had not yet arrived at the B&B. This was no small problem as it was very difficult to go on our bicycling trip without bicycles. I realize that this could be construed as a very poor attitude, but bicycles really are *the* integral part of our trips. I had arranged for the bikes to be shipped from Glendorn where we had left them the year before.

Alexandria Bay, New York, is about a six hour drive from Bradford. The bicycles were shipped out the first week of August and our trip was scheduled to start August 21st. Almost three weeks had gone by and not a bike in sight. To complicate matters, it was the summer of the UPS strike.

Our plane left too early the next morning for me to head-up the investigation, so I put some trusty souls in charge of finding our bicycles. In 1997, locating shipped items through tracking numbers was not yet available to consumers.

During our lay-over in Chicago I was told that the bicycles were to be delivered to our B&B that day. Sharon and I were only moderately encouraged. Were they really our bicycles or two they just found lying around? Will they really be delivered, and in what condition? So it was with more than a little concern that we headed into Alexandria Bay.

The town is located on the shores of the St. Lawrence River in the Thousand Island Region, and our B&B was situated close to the river. As we pulled into the driveway, we saw what could have been bicycle boxes at one time, assuming you had a vivid imagination. They looked like they had fallen off a truck, and in trying to retrieve them, they had been accidentally run over. Another possibility was that the boxes were temporarily used for hand-grenade targets. Robert Bach met us at the door. He glanced at the box remains, shook his head and could only comment, "that was how they arrived."

106

Sharon and I quickly changed into repair and rescue attire. Carefully, we removed the cardboard which sort-of encased the bicycles. At first glance everything looked alright except that there was no air in the tires, which was to be expected since we deflated them last year at the end of our trip. Once we started to put the bicycles back together, however, we realized that we were missing a few parts. Apparently, with so many holes in the cardboard, some of the disassembled pieces snuck out. With our trusty tool and repair bag we were able to overcome most of the shortages.

In the past we've had leftover parts which we always kept in case we ever figured out where they went. Sharon was missing an unidentifiable part needed to secure her handlebars to the neck of her bicycle....at least we assumed she was missing a part. It was possible, however, that we had not assembled the neck correctly. We could get it tight, but soon it worked itself loose, which meant her handlebars twisted out of line.

I know that bicycles are not complicated, but I actually do have an excuse for our apparent incompetence, weak though it may be. This was the first year we had the bicycles shipped to our B&B. Since we did not pack up the bicycles how were we to know how to put them back together? Like I said...weak! Since Alexandria Bay did not have a bicycle shop, we just did the best we could, which is to say that over the next few days we continued to keep an eye out for a bicycle shop.

Once the bicycles were more or less reassembled, we walked them into town to put air in the tires. Once the tires were inflated, we toured around to make adjustments.

By this time we were famished. In Alexandria Bay we discovered an incredible restaurant. They served fresh lobster for a very reasonable price. Now, Sharon and I *really* love lobster. We ate there each night we were in Alexandria Bay.

After our lobster dinner we walked along the shore looking out over the St. Lawrence River. A few boats moved up and down the river while lights from the island homes danced on the moving water.

The Mohawks called the St. Lawrence Kaniatarowanenneh or "big waterway." The river extends 2300 miles, connecting the Atlantic with Lake Ontario, and it is the primary drainage of the Great Lakes Basin. Part of the river forms the international boundary between Canada and the United States. The shores were originally inhabited by the Iroquois. Many explorers visited the area but found the river impassable at the Lachine rapids. With the opening of the Lachine Canal in 1825, ships could then reach Lake Ontario by way of the St. Lawrence. An extensive system of canals and locks, known as the St. Lawrence Seaway, permit ocean-going ships to pass all the way to Lake Superior. At the international border between New York and Ontario is the Thousand Island Region of the St. Lawrence. This amazing stretch of river has close to 1800 granite islands covered with white pine, oak and hemlock. By the 1800's the region had become popular among naturalists and serious sport fishermen. In the late 1800's wealthy industrialists and entrepreneurs built lavish homes on the islands.

The entire region is remarkable and, despite the shipping and assembly problems with our bikes, we were excited about our trip. At least I was, but I did not have the swiveling handlebar problem that Sharon had.

August 21st

The next morning we rode north on Route 12 as we headed for Ogdensburg, New York. Route 12 runs along the shores of the St. Lawrence River. The shoulders are extra-wide which allowed Sharon and me to ride next to each other without the fear of being flattened by cars and trucks. With a flat road, we made the forty miles to Ogdensburg in excellent time.

As we rode I noticed large fields of lovely, tall plants with yellow flowers. I also noticed Sharon coughing and sneezing continuously. She has allergies, but why is a mystery to me. I have never had allergies and do not want them....they are way too much bother. Apparently, the yellow flowers in the fields were goldenrods, which are not friendly to people with allergies.

Sharon was subjected to fits of coughing as we biked along, and she was not very lady-like about the noises she made. The coughs and sneezes were loud enough to knock your socks off! I kept a close eye on her so that when a fit came I could be prepared and not be startled off the road. I had no idea that goldenrod could be so much trouble! When the fits first began I looked at her and with a straight face commented " oh no, consumption!"

During our childhood I took great delight in taking advantage of Sharon's gullible and naïve nature to convince her of all kinds of horrible things. At one time I even had her convinced that I was a werewolf, and since they were known to attack those that they cared about, she needed to be alert when the moon was full. During the next full moon Mom found her sleeping on the floor in the hall, as if that was going to save her. I did mention how naïve she is.

Sharon had not heard the term "consumption" before, but it sounded bad and she was immediately fearful that she had some horrible disease. After all, I was her older sister and did have some medical experience. I quickly explained that it was the old fashion term for tuberculosis and that I was only kidding, and that she did not have the disease... at least I was pretty sure she didn't. Perhaps I shouldn't have added that last comment, but I couldn't resist. She is my sister, after all.

For some reason Sharon found the word consumption funny, at least in reference to her allergies. Part of the humor was relief in knowing she did not really have a terminal condition. Over the next few days as we biked along the countryside, whenever someone coughed we would look at each other, shake our heads sadly, and say "consumption." After we made our medical diagnosis, we would giggle. With all the goldenrod around, we encountered many people hacking and coughing. As the days passed, and the more we commented on people's coughs, the funnier the word consumption became. We almost could not get the word out before we started laughing. We are so easily entertained!

During our bicycling adventures we found that each year there would be one or two words, phrases, or events that really struck us as funny and would be a common thread that we would enjoy throughout the trip. This year it was the word consumption.

Ogdensburg, located on the banks of the St. Lawrence, was founded as the French Fort "La Presentation" in 1749. To keep it out of British hands, the town was destroyed by the French in 1760. Nevertheless, the British did end up occupying the area and soon rebuilt the town, which became an important military stronghold during the revolution.

The Custom House, built in 1809-1819 and located at 127 Water Street, is the oldest federal government building in the United States. Ogdensburg is also the home of the Frederic Remington Art Museum, which was why Sharon and I included the town in our trip. Both of us admire his illustrations and bronzes.

We had booked rooms at the Stonefence Inn and, although the name was enticing, it turned out to be a typical motel, not a B&B. It was perfectly pleasant, but motels are not where we like to stay. We had become accustomed to being spoiled while surrounded by charming elegance. Moreover, where was our much-needed home cooked breakfast? The motel did not have any place to put our bicycles for the night, so they ended up in our room. This arrangement was not ideal, but it was comforting to know that if anyone wanted to break into our room they would first have to tangle with two bicycles. The commotion would undoubtedly wake us up in time to throw something at them if they had not already been scared off by the ferocious bikes.

After we arrived at the motel and had stowed our gear in our room, we headed for the Art Museum. The mission of the Frederic Remington Art Museum is to "collect, exhibit, preserve and interpret the art and archives of the artist." Remington is considered one of the premier western artists in America. He was born in 1861, and his family moved to Ogdensburg in 1873. He made his name as an illustrator, mostly of western and military subjects. During the 1880s and 1890s, he illustrated for *Harper's Weekly*, *Harper's Monthly*, *Boys' Life*, *Collier's* and *Cosmopolitan*. In 1895 Remington began to create bronze sculptures, producing twenty-two subjects. He worked mainly with clay and then had them cast in bronze at art foundries. By 1898 he was working exclusively with a foundry that used the lost-wax casting method. Remington died in 1909 of complications from an appendectomy. He was only forty-eight years old.

At dinner that night we made an unfortunate discovery. The county we were staying in was dry, which meant no alcohol. Here we were in Ogdensburg, at a motel, without a beer to soothe our sore and tired muscles. Even though it had been an easy ride, our leg muscles were none too happy. They had become accustomed to better treatment and enjoyed being relaxed as the beer eased the tension and lactic acid that had built up during the day's ride. Thank goodness the trip from Alexandria Bay had not included any steep mountains! To confirm our beer theory, the next morning we did experience some soreness and stiffness.

August 22nd

As we headed out the next morning I was somewhat dismayed to learn that rain was expected. Even more disconcerting was that our route took us directly east toward the Adirondacks. As I studied the map, I hoped we would only reach the foothills. We did not want to bicycle in the Adirondacks. Lake Placid is in the Adirondacks, and the 1980 Winter Olympics were held there. Remember "the miracle on ice" by the US hockey team? Well, the Winter Olympics mean mountains, really high mountains, for skiing and other winter sports.

Our destination was Potsdam which is not part of the designated Adirondack Park. We just hoped that in delineating the Park, all the mountains were included within its boundaries and that one or two had not escaped, particularly around Potsdam.

Before reaching Potsdam we traveled through Canton, New York. As we rode through the town we found the bicycle shop which had eluded us until now. The name of the shop was the Bicycle Post and the guys running it were great. They whipped Sharon's bike into the back and within a few minutes fixed the handlebar problem for a whopping charge of $10.69. While someone worked on the bike, Sharon and I visited with one of the clerks. Bicyclists from all over frequent Canton and the surrounding area for the bicycling experiences and races. Understandingly, he touted the Adirondacks as great bicycling and encouraged us to give them a try, if not this year than some other time. We made note of his youth and incredibly strong looking legs. As of yet "some other time" has not happened.

From Canton we had a choice of taking the longer way on Route 68 to 56 and then into Potsdam, or taking the shorter way on Route 11, which took us straight into town. For several reasons we chose the shorter route:

1. Rain was threatening.
2. It was shorter.
3. The longer route took us further into the Adirondacks.
4. Our legs, in an effort to get back at us for depriving them of a beer

tonic the night before, were inflicting us with pain.

5. Sharon was in the last stages of consumption.

6. It was shorter. (This top priority needed repeating)

As the rain started we knew the shorter route had been the right choice. Is it ever the wrong choice?

Potsdam was founded in 1803 by Benjamin Raymond. The schoolhouse he built later became part of the State University in 1949. Another family, the Clarksons, also settled in the area and ran a number of businesses, built Trinity Church and founded the Thomas Clarkson Memorial College of Technology which was built of sandstone from the local quarry. Sandstone from the area was used in structures as far away as Ottawa, Syracuse and New York City.

We stayed at the Clarkson Inn, which also turned out not to be a Bed and Breakfast, but a rather nice hotel.

With the rain continuing and a theater just across the street, we decided to go to the movies. Sharon and I love movies and popcorn, and not necessarily in that order. That night we saw Harrison Ford in "Air Force One." Good popcorn, good movie!

August 23rd

The next day it was still raining. Actually, it was closer to wet air. Our hotel overlooked Ives Park, located on the bank of the Raquette River. The picture on the front cover was taken at the park. We couldn't resist the extra decorations for our bikes, as if we did not have enough to carry.

From Potsdam we headed west to the Ogdensburg bridge where we crossed over the St. Lawrence into Ontario, Canada. The bridge is constructed of metal grates instead of a solid surface. Now, this presented a problem. I have a real fear of bridges, but am terrified of any that have grates. I will not walk over a grate of any kind. If there is one in a sidewalk or in a road, I go around it. We faced a critical situation:

1. It was still raining, which makes for slippery roads.

2. Sharon, although better, was still dealing with consumption and was not herself. Maybe she was also allergic to the sunflowers which were part of our bicycle decorations.

3. I have a serious bridge phobia.

4. Automobiles use the bridge.

Unfortunately, cars were crossing over the bridge while we were on it. Due to the rain there were areas where we actually hydroplaned, causing us to slip and slide, which was hard to understand with all the weight we were carrying.

In order for me to bike across any bridge, grated or not, I have to follow

Sharon and look at the back of her bicycle. At no time can I take my eyes off the back, and absolutely no looking at the water so many feet below. If at any time I lose focus, I tighten up and lose speed causing the bike to start to wobble back and forth. My pedaling gets all out of whack. When the wobbling gets bad enough I am in danger of going into traffic or off the edge, so I have to stop to regain control. To this day I have not been able to overcome this disastrous reaction.

Because of the conditions, Sharon also had quite a bit of trouble keeping a straight, steady pace. Fortunately, she had not mentioned this while we were on the bridge. If she had slid into the traffic or off the bridge I would have just followed right behind her. The absolute worst thing Sharon and I can do in tense situations is to talk. For us, moments of fear lead to laughter, which worsens the "wobble effect."

In complete silence, and after what seemed like hours, we reached the Canadian side. We had to take a break in order for us to calm our racing hearts. The traumatic crossing was quickly dissipated by laughter. As noted before, fear is followed by the healing elixir of laughter.

So it was with some mirth and relief that we approached the customs booth, totally unprepared for the upcoming exchange which needed a crystal-clear head. I am not sure if the problem with customs was because the agent was new at his job, or that he just kept asking the wrong questions. It is possible that our answers could have contributed ever-so-slightly to the confusion. After all, we were in a fragile emotional state having just survived a harrowing crossing of the St. Lawrence.

The confusion began when we biked up to the booth. The agent was obviously not accustomed to bicyclists coming up to his window. Our sunflower and cattail decorations probably didn't help. Once we were at the booth, he asked where we were from. This was his first and last good question. At the time, we were living in Texas, although in different parts of the state.

"Texas," we answered in unison. The agent, a fairly young man, should have stopped with that question but, apparently confused, he pressed on.

"You bicycled all the way from Texas!?"

"No," we both answered.

"So you are not from Texas."

"Yes, we are from Texas."

"Well, how did you get here?"

"On our bicycles."

"But you said you didn't bicycle from Texas."

"We didn't." (Where did they get this guy?)

"How did you get here from Texas?"

"We flew into Syracuse."

"So you bicycled from Syracuse?"

"No, from Potsdam."

"Is that where you started from?"

"No, we started at Alexandria Bay."

The exchange went on for a while longer, and was very reminiscent of the old Abbott and Costello "who's on first" routine. Sharon and I found this whole exchange *really* funny, which we know did not help with the interrogation. I am sure the agent expected us to show more respect. Finally, in complete frustration, the agent gave up and asked how long we were going to be in Canada. Actually, this was not a bad question and was probably required. We told him "a couple of days" which, from his reaction, was a couple of days too many. Since we were staying overnight, he asked where we were staying while in Canada. We said "in Brockville." Before he waved us on, he asked if we were planning to return to the U.S. via this bridge. I told him we were to re-enter the U.S. at the International Bridge farther south. His expression of pure relief was a little disconcerting. He had asked the questions, not us. Maybe the sunflowers were too distracting.

As we headed for Brockville, about twenty miles to the south, Sharon and I were grateful that we had made it over the bridge, but probably more impressive is that we got past the customs agent.

Our route took us along the banks of the St. Lawrence toward Brockville. The rain had become a light drizzle, but still wet. Rain, regardless of intensity, is always wet when one is on a bike. The roads were narrow, with very little shoulder in spots, but the traffic was relatively light.

We stopped in Prescott for lunch. We were wearing our bright pink balloon T-shirts with the matching socks that Sharon had modified. She had sewn real, un-inflated balloons onto our hot pink socks. The balloons were attached so that the opening was at the top. There were five balloons, all of different colors. I thought it was very clever and was a proper compliment to our T-shirts.

During lunch Sharon confessed that she was concerned about the balloons on our socks. She was worried that the balloons would fill with water and therefore cause pedaling problems. It was an interesting vision. I imagined the balloons slowly filing with water until we both had 3 to 4 inch diameter water balloons hanging off our ankles. When I realized she was serious I quickly eased her concern, telling her that the balloons would more than likely break off before they caused any trouble. However, I could tell Sharon had started to lose her enthusiasm for our balloon socks.

We had our rain jackets on, so the other lunch patrons were unable to see our matching T-shirts. They could see our socks, though, and we noticed that while we were in the restaurant most of the patrons kept glancing our way. As we were leaving the restaurant a young boy of about 11 years old came up to us. He had

113

been with one of the families that had taken a particular interest in us. He said his family wanted to know why there were balloons sewn on our socks. I explained how they were part of our bicycling outfit and that they matched our T-shirts. Apparently my explanation made no impression. In utter confusion, he left to report back to his family. I couldn't imagine why it was so complicated. After he left Sharon decided that the balloon socks had to go and became rather adamant about it. As convinced as she was at the time, we were to wear them again, with very comical results.

A few miles to the north of Brockville we passed our Bed and Breakfast. Made of stone, it did not have the inviting warmth that so many of our B&Bs were known for. With eyes of eagles, we noticed that there were not any restaurants near our B&B. Although tired and wet after having had a fairly stressful day dealing with rain, a scary bridge, balloon socks and a customs agent, Sharon and I decided we had better head into town for something to eat and to find a beer. Make that a six-pack.

You see, our beer needs are a direct result of the kind of day we have on our bikes. The more stressful the day, and the harder or longer the ride, the more beer we need to overcome the trauma. Although we rarely drink more than one or possibly two beers each evening, over the years we have made it through some tough situations by rating our challenges in terms of beers to be consumed. This imagined beer feast is sort of the carrot-in-front-of-the-donkey, or reward at the end of the trail. For example, each morning, being fresh, we would say that this was a one-beer day. If the route was particularly tough, by noon we might be at a six-pack, and by evening it could be up to two six packs or higher. Regardless of how many beers the rating called for, we still only drank one or two. It was the idea, that somehow was very comforting.

Brockville is one of the oldest cities in Ontario and was named for the War of 1812 British hero, Sir Isaac Brock. The lavish home of Senator George T. Fulford, who made his fortune with "Pink Pills for Pale People" (you can actually find this on the internet), is in Brockville. With nearby sunken ships remaining from the War of 1812, Brockville is an excellent area to scuba dive.

As we entered this charming town the rain intensified and was still wet (go figure!). By that time we were miserable! We bought a pizza-to-go at the first place we came to and found some beer at a convenience store. We hurried back to our B&B. Once inside, we quickly gobbled down our pizza, drank our beer and went to bed. We were just plain whipped.

August 24th

All too soon we had come to the last day of our bicycling journey. Although a little windy, the day was bright and sunny. At Brockville we entered the twenty-five mile paved pathway that runs next to the Thousand Island Parkway, connecting Brockville with Gananoque.

We were enjoying the tranquil ride along the shores of the St. Lawrence when, in the distance, we could hear a faint roar. "What in the world...?" I was sure there were not any falls along this part of the St. Lawrence. As we continued to ride south the noise level increased. We were befuddled as to the cause until, around the bend in front of us, a large number of speed boats appeared. They were racing along the St. Lawrence at incredible speeds. We hoped this was an event of some kind and not a daily summer outing. What noise! I do not know how the crews could handle the high-pitched whine the engines made in an effort to go so fast. So much for the peace and quiet of back country bicycling!

When we stopped for lunch we found out that this was the annual Power Boating Magazine Poker Run held every August. The object of the poker run was for the boats to go to several predetermined locations and pick up a playing card. Once all the required cards had been picked up, the boat headed for the finish line. Crews come from all over to participate in the race. Each crew had a support team and/or family that helped out or came to enjoy the event. Usually, each team had a name and identifying colors.

As it turned out, Sharon and I unknowingly had chosen to wear our playing card outfits that day. Our T-shirts showed the four suits in black and red on a white background. We fit right in and everyone concluded we were part of a team.

We continued along the St. Lawrence to the International Bridge where we had planned to cross back over to the U.S. It was still early, however, and since it was only eleven miles on a paved bikeway, Sharon and I decided to proceed to Gananoque. The town is known as "The Canadian Gateway to the 1000 Islands" and means "town on two rivers." In addition to hosting the Poker Run, the town features one of Eastern Ontario's largest celebrations, the Festival of the Islands.

Having rained the day before, it was muggy and hot. Although the bikeway was flat and we were pedaling away, we only averaged around six to eight miles an hour. I was very discouraged. We thought we should be able to make better time and not be so worn out. My legs were toast!

Eventually we limped into Gananoque and headed for the Historic 1000 Islands Village located on the St. Lawrence River. It took a while to learn how to pronounce Gananoque (Gan-uh-Nock-way), but once we learned how to say it we felt like natives. We were told by the locals that they could identify the tourists by how they mispronounced the name of their town.

Immediately after our bikes were locked up we purchased an iced coffee which tasted soooo good. For some reason we craved an iced coffee, which is not something we normally drink. Isn't it remarkable how every so often you eat or drink something that just hits the spot and the memory of that delightful moment stays with you?

After we finished our coffee, we wandered around the village where we purchased red Canadian T-shirts for a future bike trip. Although I knew in my heart that Ouisi would not be joining us for any future trips, we bought her one just in case.

After spending an hour or two in the village, I felt that we needed to start back. Our journey into Gananoque had taken so long and I wanted us to have plenty of time to get back into the U.S. Besides, I was very apprehensive about the bridge crossing and just wanted to get it over with.

With renewed energy we headed back to the bridge. Whoa.... what happened? Sharon and I were flying down the road at twenty-plus miles per hour with little effort. Our legs were working like well-oiled pistons. There was no way the coffee could have made that much difference! I could not figure out what was going on. It was as if we were being pushed along. Of course....that was it. We were being pushed along by the wind. Our slow progress heading into Gananoque was due to a strong head-wind and not our pathetic biking ability. What a relief!

The best way to describe the impact of the tail-wind is to compare it to the difference between unaided walking and how effortless it is to walk on a moving sidewalk like the ones you find at some airports. We went from feeling like little old ladies to young athletes in a matter of hours. What a ride...it was one of our best.

Within minutes we arrived at the International Bridge which crosses over Canadian Hill Island and American Wellesley Island to connect Ontario's Highway 401 to U.S. Interstate 81. Being a major thoroughfare, there was quite a line waiting to get through customs. I noticed that we were the only ones on bicycles.

Knowing we were going into Canada before we started our trip, I was informed that we only needed a driver's license to cross back into the U.S. We dismounted and walked along as the line moved forward. Since the line was moving slowly I took the opportunity to get my license out of my pack. While retrieving it I noticed that the car behind us was full of extra-cute guys. Good looking men are always appreciated. Sharon was in front of me, so I called to her to go ahead and get her license ready. It is important to remember that we bungeed everything to a rack on the back of our bikes. All of our gear has to go there. We have learned that under no circumstances do not, let me repeat, do not ever let your bike fall over. With so much bungeed onto the bike rack, the back was very top-heavy and prone to falling over. When the bikes fall over, everything on the back slides to the side and must be re-bungeed. This was always so frustrating because it inevitably took a couple of tries before we got the correct distribution and balance.

To keep her bike stable Sharon had both hands on her handlebar. To reach her purse she had to let go of the far-side handlebar. The back of her bike was weighted down with her gear, so without both hands on the front handlebar, the back started to fall over. In an effort to keep the bike upright she grabbed the handlebar with both hands again, but the back was still falling. Since she could not take her hands off the handlebar, she pushed forward to try to keep the bike upright, but the weight in the back pulled the bike to the side. If she stopped moving, the bike would fall over. The conflicting forces resulted in her running in a circle like a dog chasing its tail. There was no question that Sharon was desperately trying to keep her bike upright, but she needed help. Who better to help than her one-and-only sister? However, I was in no position to lend a hand, having plopped down on the ground, laughing so hard at the sight of her chasing her bicycle. I couldn't stand up, let alone help her.

In the end the bike won and crashed to the ground. In hysterics, Sharon just sat down next to her bike. It took a few minutes before I was able to get up. As I stood, I happened to notice the car behind us with the good looking guys. They were doubled over with laughter. Fortunately the line was moving slowly, for I doubted that the driver was in any condition to steer the car.

When I turned back around I saw Sharon lying on her back. Her gear was a mess. Between us, although slowed by bouts of laughter, we reassembled her gear onto her bike. Taking no chances, I held her bike as she retrieved her license.

Ten years passed before I dared to ask her why she hadn't put down her kickstand before she reached for her license. When I did ask, there was silence. Well, I think enough said.

As our turn came to approach the customs booth, I noticed that the guys behind us were still laughing. I completely understood. When the customs agent saw our driver's licenses clutched in our outstretched hands, he told us they were not necessary. Sharon, normally a kind and forgiving person, gave me an indescribable look of disgust. At that moment she could easily have been contemplating my quick demise. While deciding the best and most painful punishment for me, she hesitated long enough to hear the agent inform us that bicycles were not allowed on the Canadian bridge due to some road construction.

Apparently our crestfallen faces, not to mention our shaky legs and the threat of tears, had the necessary impact on the agent. He quickly told us not to worry... he would get us a ride. With immense relief we took our bikes off to the side while we waited for a wonderful angel to come to our rescue. We never doubted one would appear because they always have in the past. The auto with the cute guys quickly passed through customs and turned into the visitor's rest area. At last sight they were still laughing.

We did not have to wait long for our angel. A truck pulled over to where we were waiting and the driver told us that he could give us a ride over the Canadian bridge to the American Wellesley Island. He quickly loaded our bikes and us into the back of the truck and off we went. I was very grateful to be getting a lift even if it was only halfway across the river. Once we arrived at Wellesley Island, the driver unloaded our bikes, and off we rode.

Wellesley Island, over 8000 acres, is located in the center of the St. Lawrence River. It is the home of both Wellesley Island State Park and Thousand Island Park. Thousand Island Park is the largest community on the island and features hundreds of Victorian homes, with some of the most beautiful architecture in the region. The Historic District is the only surviving example of the late 19th century religious colonies left in the 1000 island region, with few changes from a century ago.

As the American bridge came into view, I knew my earlier anxieties were well-founded. The bridge was the worst of nightmares for someone with my bridge phobia. With a span of 4500ft. and an under-clearance of 150ft., it is very long and high. There was lots of traffic and as the many trucks and cars passed over the bridge, it shook. To further add to my mounting anxiety, the bridge was grated. Even though there was a separate pedestrian walkway, it appeared to be hanging off the edge of the bridge. There was no way I was going to be able to do this. I told Sharon to save herself and go on. Taking pity on me, Sharon put aside the license incident and told me we would cross together. She assured me the success of the crossing would certainly warrant at least two six-packs of beer, which was easy for her to say since we knew she would get across.

Frankly, I could have used one six-pack just to make the crossing. Well... maybe two six-packs. Slowly, we started across. The pedestrian path was really too narrow to bike, which I could not have done anyway. Even though I was walking, I still needed to focus on the back of Sharon's bike. Every time a truck went by I froze while the bridge shook. I had no idea there were so many trucks in the world, and never figured out why they were all crossing the St. Lawrence while I was on the bridge. Throughout the entire crossing I never looked down or even out at the water.

Apparently there are few places that rival the panoramic view of the region as seen from the International Bridge. Absolutely nothing Sharon said could get me to take a look, so she took a picture instead. A postcard would have done just as well. My sixth sense shouted to me that it was a long way down, and my worst fears were confirmed when I later saw the picture she took.

Sharon was great. She kept up a steady conversation, reminding me to stay focused on the back of her bike and the two six-packs of beer we would enjoy to celebrate the crossing. I told her if I didn't make it to be sure a have a beer or three for me. Seriously, I really was terrified and pretty shaky.

Apparently this was the view from the bridge over the St Lawrence

Once across, I had to lie down for a while to recover. Then, as usual, I was overcome with laughter. The greater the fear and tension, the harder and longer the laughter. I lay there laughing for a long time.

Just where the bridge reached the American mainland was Mazeland. The maze was made out of tall bushes and very reminiscent of the ones seen in England and Europe. I have always been fascinated with the old estate mazes and have thought it would be so much fun to explore one. Just when I was in such a desperate state and in need of some kind of diversion, a maze appears. Maybe that is why the maze was located at the bottom of the bridge…to help pedestrians and motorists recover from the crossing. Along with the extended laughing fit, the maze was just what I needed to put the fearsome bridge incident behind me.

After we explored the maze, where we got lost many times, we headed back to Alexandria Bay. Before going to our B&B we stopped at a convenience store to get our well-deserved beer. Because of the fun and adventure of the maze, we only needed to purchase one six-pack. Back at the B&B, we cleaned up for dinner, but before heading to the restaurant we had a beer on the porch while overlooking the St. Lawrence. We returned to the porch for a second beer after our lobster dinner.

Our bicycle journey was over for this year, and the next day we had to head home. The evening was gorgeous and we paused to thank God for our safe trip and to toast our exciting bike adventure. I was particularly thankful that I had survived *THE BRIDGE*.

August 25th

After breakfast we had to face-up to packing our bikes, which proved to be somewhat of a challenge. We only had the boxes that they had arrived in and they were in pretty bad shape considering that they had been used for hand-grenade practice. Strapping tape is now a required item for all our bike trips.

Since our plane did not leave until the afternoon, Sharon and I took the opportunity to tour the famous Boldt Castle, which was built on Hart Island in the St. Lawrence River. We took the ferry over to the island. The property had been acquired by The Thousand Islands Bridge Authority with the understanding that all revenues would be used to restore the castle in order to preserve it for the enjoyment of future generations. The tour offered a film about the life of George Boldt and the history of the castle.

While waiting for the film to begin, we toured the castle and the beautifully landscaped grounds. The castle had never been finished and was in the process of being restored. As soon as the theatre doors opened Sharon and I quickly took our seats, eager to learn more about the island and the man who wanted to build a castle. Holding about fifty metal seats divided down the middle by an aisle, the theatre was almost full when the film started.

George Boldt was born in Prussia in 1851 and immigrated to America when he was a teenager. In 1876 he was hired to work at the famous "Philadelphia Club" in Philadelphia, Pa. George fell in love with Louise Kehrer, whose father owned the club. He and Louise were the perfect match, and in 1877 they were married. He went on to become the most successful hotel magnate in America, managing the Waldorf-Astoria Hotel in New York City, while owning the Bellevue-Stratford in Philadelphia. He ran both hotels until his death in 1916.

George helped revolutionize the hotel business with the concept of room service, free newspapers for each guest, and together with Louise, was instrumental in the growth and success of both hotels. Over the years George acquired many properties in and around the St. Lawrence River. He absolutely adored his wife and family, and to honor his love for his cherished Louise, he planned to build a castle on Hart Island and present it to her on Valentine's Day, her birthday.

In 1900 he began the ambitious construction of the castle, which was to be one of the largest private homes in America. All work was to be done by the finest artists and master craftsmen to be found. Heart motifs were placed throughout the castle to signify his love for Louise. When she died suddenly in 1904 all construction stopped, and George Boldt never returned to the island. The unfinished castle was abandoned for seventy-three years.

George was totally devastated by Louise's death. According to the film, no one knew for sure the cause of death, but it had been speculated that she died of consumption.

The result of that statement was disastrous for Sharon and me. The timing could not have been worse, or better, depending on how you look at it. At the most emotional point of the film, Sharon and I heard the word "consumption," the one word we had spent the last five days repeating and having fun with. The coincidence was beyond explanation. We took one look at each other and burst into laughter. We were laughing so hard we actually slid off our seats. We knew we had to get out of the theatre, and get out fast! Since we couldn't stand up, we actually crawled up the aisle to exit the theatre. As we reached the theatre doors, we were able to stand. After exiting the theatre we quickly headed for the ladies room to hide out.

Who could have known that a pretty, yellow weed would cause so much trouble?

**1998**
**Approximately** 175 miles

Route ● ● ● ● ● ● ● ● ● ● ●

Highways _____

Chapter 9
1998

"It's Not the Socks"

August 11th

For our ninth year Sharon and I planned to continue our exploration of the St. Lawrence and Thousand Island regions, both on the American and Canadian sides, including a visit to Kingston, Ontario, Canada. We agreed to return to the area only under the following conditions:

1. I absolutely refused to consider crossing the St. Lawrence over a bridge, at least not the long, shaky, grated kind. Once in a lifetime was once too much. The alternative was to cross by water. As it turned out, there was a daily ferry service provided to take autos, pedestrians and bicyclists over to Kingston. Perfect!

2. In addition, Sharon insisted that the word "consumption" be banned from our vocabulary. She had allergies, not some horrible disease. She received no argument from me, as I re-lived the embarrassment of last year's tour of Boldt castle. With that incident in mind we wisely chose not include a return trip to Alexandria Bay as part of this year's agenda. Because of the fabulous lobster we had at the Alexandria Bay restaurant, this was not as easy a decision as it should have been.

Our trip started in Oswego, New York, located on the shores of Lake Ontario. We had booked a room at the Oswego Inn. The area around Oswego was first visited by the French Explorer Samuel de Champlain in 1615. In 1722 the British established a trading post in the area, which was later fortified and named Fort Oswego. In 1755 Fort Ontario was added on the northeast side of the Oswego River. The Oswego Canal, a branch of the Erie Canal, reached the area in 1829.

During World War II Oswego was home to almost one thousand Jewish refugees. Fort Ontario was the only place America provided as a shelter for Jewish refugees during that war. Oswego calls itself "The Port City of Central New York."

August 12th

Unlike last year, the weather forecast for our trip was perfect. There was no rain predicted, with temperatures around the eighties and, even more importantly, the humidity was to be relatively low. Sharon and I really do not like very humid days because it saps our energy. Combine high temperatures with high humidity and it is easy for a bicyclist to get into trouble. Sharon and I certainly didn't need any help getting into trouble...we seemed to accomplish that on our own.

We did not leave Oswego until late morning. The first day of each trip usually took longer to get started since we had to get all of our gear organized and our bikes assembled and adjusted.

Since early settlers founded towns near low-lying water sources such as a lake or river, Sharon and I have learned that we usually have to negotiate a hill upon leaving a town. But in turn, we quite often have a hill to go down as we entered a town for the last leg of the day. Just to clarify, "last leg" refers to our legs as well as a part of the journey.

So, it didn't come as a surprise that as we left Oswego on Route 3, heading north to Sackets Harbor, we had to bike up a hill. Just as we were to start up the hill Sharon had a flat. Sharon over the years seems to have flats on a regular basis. We have actually become quite proficient at changing out tubes, even the back one. Continuing on, I noted that road had very narrow shoulders with a two to three foot-deep culvert on the side. The culvert had a cement bottom, but otherwise had grass and vegetation on its sides.

With my bike in the lowest gear and over thirty pounds of stuff bungeed on the back, I had a great deal of trouble maintaining enough speed to keep my bike heading straight along the edge of the road. Bicyclists with powerful legs will have no idea what I am trying to describe. Because I am unable to maintain enough speed, I start to wobble left and right. The steeper the hill, the more I wobble. Then I start to laugh. I suppose this comes from my mental image of what it must look like as I wobble up each hill. If there is a fairly wide shoulder, I do not have this problem, which leads me to believe that I have some minor psychological block. With only a six-inch white line separating me from the cars speeding by on my left and the culvert on my right, I knew I was battling a lost cause. I was either going to go left into the traffic or end up in the ditch.

Like a black hole, the culvert slowly pulled me towards it. When I spotted a particularly soft looking section of grass up ahead, I finally gave up and just steered my bike into the culvert to get it over with. Sharon, along with the people in the car that were just getting ready to pass us, saw me disappear over the side and into the culvert. Having purposely chosen my exit from the road, I landed on grass while the bike took the brunt of the cement section.

Sharon hurried to see if I was alright, but having experienced eight years of biking with me she had a pretty good idea of what had happened and figured I was fine. Not that I have gone into ditches before, but she had seen my signature wobble while going up hills, followed by my head dropping down in what she calls my vulture position which is what happens when I start laughing. She knew I was eventually going to end up in the ditch. I suppose she experienced some concern for a brief moment, but it was soon replaced with laughter as she saw me stand up.

Although I had some grass stains, along with one or two small cuts, I was fine. The bicycle was an entirely different matter. The seat and handlebar were askew, and my gear was all over the place.

In the meantime the driver of the car that was about to pass me when I disappeared over the edge, quickly stopped. As a witness they probably felt that they would be needed in the rescue. They could help direct the helicopter, which I was surely going to need to transport me to the nearest trauma center, to the site of the accident. However, when I popped up so quickly with all the appearances of being in one piece, they proceeded on. Since Sharon and I were both laughing, they probably felt it best not to get involved. Sharon was on the grass in hysterics, not because of the relief in seeing me in one piece, but because she said that watching me wobble up the hill doing my vulture imitation, and then disappearing into the ditch, was like a Keystone Cop comedy. It was funny, and I was laughing too, but not *that* funny. I mean, I was bleeding. With great mirth, she just rolled around in the grass.

Eventually she composed herself enough to lend a hand, although she proved to be of little help since she had to frequently stop for bouts of laughter, at which time I would point to my bleeding leg. That didn't seem to help though, because she kept reliving the vision of me going into the ditch. To further complicate matters, there was little space to maneuver with no shoulder, speeding cars on one side, and the ditch on the other. Consequently, it took some time to gather my gear and properly re-bungee it onto the bike. Once I had put everything back together and made the necessary adjustments, I walked up the rest of the hill in the culvert.

We continued along the shore of Lake Ontario, taking as many of the shore roads as we could in order to enjoy the lake.

We had made reservations at the Old Stone Row Country Inn in Sackets Harbor. The town was founded by a New York City Lawyer, Augustus Sackets. It sits on one of the largest natural harbors on Lake Ontario, close to where the St. Lawrence joins the lake, and is less than 30 miles from Canada.

Because of its strategic location, Sackets Harbor became the center of military and naval operations for the northern theater during the War of 1812. At the time it was America's single largest naval port and shipbuilding center. It was at Sackets Harbor that the largest American fleet of the war was constructed. Due to its military significance, two battles were fought at Sackets Harbor during the War of 1812. Both battles were won by the Americans, but not without the town sustaining considerable damage. After the War of 1812, Madison Barracks was built, which contributed to the post-war boom and transformed the crude barrack town of tents and log shanties into a village of considerable elegance, with dignified Federal-style buildings.

By the second half of the 1800's, the entire Thousand Island Region, including Sackets Harbor, became popular as a seasonal resort, bringing the first of many summer visitors to Lake Ontario's scenic shores. Unfortunately, the decade after WW II brought the demise of the lake trade along with the abandonment of not only the railroad, but also Madison Barracks and the Naval Station. Today, Sackets Harbor enjoys revitalization as a quaint tourist resort community.

The Old Stone Row Country Inn is part of the old Madison Barracks. The 125 acre barracks and surrounding land are now privately owned. Madison Barracks, acclaimed as a living museum of military architecture, has played a part in every war involving our nation from the War of 1812 through World War II.

The Inn dates back to 1816-1819, and overlooks Lake Ontario. We had a lovely dinner on the grounds of Madison Barracks in one of the old buildings which had been converted into a restaurant. As we prepared for bed, I would not have been the least surprised to have heard taps being played.

August 13th

The Inn did not provide breakfast, so we were directed to a restaurant nearby and it was fabulous, with an incredible menu. Everything Sharon and I love was on it, along with many other delicious-sounding dishes. Where to begin! With so many wonderful offerings, just choosing a dish was a problem. We ordered several items just to be able to try as many dishes as possible. I would have to say that we pretty much waddled to our bikes after finishing our meal.

From Sackets Harbor we headed toward the St. Lawrence and our crossing-point into Canada. We chose to wear our hot-pink balloon T-shirts that day. You might remember that these were the outfits that have socks with matching balloons sewn on them. Sharon really did not want to wear the socks, but I insisted because, for one thing, they so cleverly matched our T-shirts, and secondly, her concerns were unfounded. Granted, it was an interesting coincidence that last year when we entered Canada we were wearing the same outfit. I assured her that the family that quizzed us about our outfits last year had to be an exception. Reluctantly, she acquiesced. With Sharon slightly uneasy about our attire, we headed for Kingston, Ontario.

Most of the road from Sackets Harbor to the ferry landing was inland and therefore not as picturesque. However, we did pass through Cape Vincent on our way to the landing, where we were to board our boat for Canada.

Cape Vincent is a small, picturesque village located at the point where the

St. Lawrence River flows into Lake Ontario. With his brother Joseph already living in Cape Vincent, Napoleon Bonaparte is said to have settled there for a time to seek refuge from the havoc he had caused in Europe.

While we waited for the ferry, Sharon and I checked out a few of the local stores. The lighthouse on Tibbets Point in Cape Vincent is one of the oldest lighthouses on the Great Lakes. Due to its presence, the stores abound with anything to do with lighthouses. They were everywhere and on everything. Although Sharon and I actually like lighthouses, we had little interest in buying a replica or clothing depicting them. Since neither of us live near an ocean, lighthouses have never made the list of the top one hundred things we must have. However, we somehow managed to purchase light pink T-shirts with lighthouses on them. This is a strong verification of how influential some marketing techniques can be. To this day we have never worn those T-shirts on one of our bicycling trips. They are too pale and…well….have lighthouses on them.

We boarded the ferry to Kingston soon after lunch, which we enjoyed on the harbor near the landing. I was looking forward to our ferry ride. No bridges to bike across! I knew it would take years to truly overcome the traumatic crossing of the Thousand Island International Bridge on last year's trip. Well….for me, more like a lifetime.

Kingston Ferry

As the ferry took us across the St. Lawrence, I leaned against the boat's railing while the wind blew across my face, and listened to the sound of water slapping against the side of the boat. The ferry ride was so delightful and the St. Lawrence so majestic.

Because the St. Lawrence is the International border between the U.S. and Canada, the American ferry stops at Wolfe Island, Canada, for everyone to disembark. From there, we headed for the dock on the north side of the island at Marysville in order to catch the Canadian ferry to Kingston. As we meandered slowly down the road, all the cars from the ferry soon passed by, allowing us to enjoy the peaceful beauty of the island.

Wolfe Island was known to the Indians as "Ganounkouesnot", meaning "Long Island Standing Up." The island is over 30,000 acres and is the largest in the Thousand Island Region.

As we boarded the Kingston ferry, I noticed Sharon's bike was listing...well, actually it was her pack. At first I thought it needed to be re-bungeed since we seem to always be adjusting our packs, but on closer inspection I saw that one of the screws that secured her bike rack onto the back axle was missing. It was evident that the weight of her pack would start to bend the rack post into her bike spokes. Having anything metal protrude into your spokes while moving is not advisable since it would cause an immediate halt to the bike and the rider would be hurled into the air. Fortunately, I found a paperclip in my fanny pack which I was able to use for this emergency. Why I would have a paperclip on a bicycle adventure is beyond me. Oh, those silly angels! When I inserted it into the screw hole, the clip appeared to secure the rack, if only temporarily. I hoped this would be good enough to get us to our B&B, and then we would look for a bike shop to fix it properly.

Kingston is among Canada's oldest settlements and that nation's first capital. Like Cape Vincent, Kingston is located at the junction of the St. Lawrence and Lake Ontario. Unlike the quaint village of Cape Vincent, Kingston is a bustling cosmopolitan city, combining history and culture with more than two dozen museums, historic sites and art galleries. Home of the sailing events at the 21st Olympic Games, Kingston has become known as the "fresh-water sailing capital of the world."

While we biked towards our B&B, I was astounded to see so many churches. They seemed to be on every corner. Most were massive stone edifices with very impressive Gothic architecture.

We stayed at the Secret Garden Bed and Breakfast the nights of the 13th and 14th. The B&B, located in downtown Kingston, was built in 1888. The gardens are beautiful, as is the home. Our hosts, John and Mary Baker, were wonderful and went out of their way to make theater and dinner reservations for us.

After leaving the ferry, we immediately looked up bicycle shops and found one close to our B&B. Once at the Secret Garden, Sharon and I unloaded our gear and quickly headed to the bike shop to get her rack repaired. As we rounded the corner of the street where the bike shop was located, I could see a few guys working on bicycles in front of a home about four houses down on the right. I pointed out the shop to Sharon.

"See the guys working on the bikes on the lawn up ahead? That must be it," I said.

Now, for all the years we have been biking, Sharon has never, I mean never, been in the lead except, of course, when she has to get me across a bridge. Just as I rounded the corner, however, Sharon shot passed me. When the shop was about a hundred feet away she started yelling at the top of her lungs, "I need a screw!"

What? Did I hear that right? Did Sharon just yell, "I need a screw?" I almost fell over in a dead faint. I quickly accelerated, yelling, "for her bike…for her bike!" Too late! The guys on the lawn all looked up with their mouths agape.

As Sharon disappeared into the shop, I decided it would be better if I stayed outside on the street. Unfortunately, because we both had on the hot pink T-shirts, the guys on the lawn concluded that I was with Sharon, an association I was not sure I wanted at that moment. Before I got there, several of the guys had already followed Sharon into the shop. After a short time, Sharon re-appeared with a new screw in place. She told me that the screw was free….no charge. Really? Imagine that!

We headed down the street and, as we rounded the next corner, we happened to glance back in time to see several of the guys bent over in laughter. Sharon just looked at me with big eyes and asked, "do you think it's our socks?" I just looked at her, shook my head and could only say, "no, it's not our socks." She was completely clueless. After we were well away from the shop, I explained to her why the guys were laughing. Even so, we never wore our balloon socks again.

We stayed in Kingston for two nights. The second night we saw "A Chorus Line." The show is one of the longest running musicals on Broadway.

We enjoyed a number of restaurants on this trip, but the names are what stick in our minds. For example, in Kingston we went to The Sleepless Goat Café, Le Caveru, and last but not least, twice to Chez Piggy, which was excellent.

August 14th

We planned a full day in Kingston to be able to tour around and venture out into the countryside without our gear. For several reasons, this proved to be very relaxing:

1. We had no gear to haul around.

2. We did not have to push to get to our next destination since we were already there.

3. It gave us a day to bike as much or as little as we felt like. In other words, this was our "Had to Take a Break" day.

4. If the weather turned bad or hills became too steep, we could just go back to our B&B.

Such nice options!

August 15th

The following day we headed back to Sackets Harbor. During a break, I noticed Sharon's gear was listing again. The new screw was missing. Now what? "Houston, we have a problem." Actually, Sharon had a problem. My bike was fine. As I glanced at the scabs on my leg from my trip into the ditch, I remembered the complete lack of sympathy she had shown during my time of need. However, Sharon looked so forlorn standing next to her listing bike. I knew I had to come up with a solution. Being fresh out of paper clips, I was at a loss as to what we could do. We had stopped in an upscale residential area, so stores were few and far between. In fact, there were none. As I considered pounding on a few doors looking for help, I noticed a piece of wire on the ground. Just got to love those angels! Not only did the wire work perfectly, but it also lasted for the rest of the trip, unlike the screw she got at the bike shop. I guess you get what you pay for.

We took our time returning to Sackets Harbor. Occasionally, we headed down country roads to explore the area and get closer to the lakeshore. There are a number of state parks along the shores of Lake Ontario and the St. Lawrence River. At Sackets Harbor, we went over to Westcott Beach State Park and sat on the shore just to watch the water and the activities on the lake. For our return trip, we had again booked a room at the Old Stone Row Country Inn.

August 16th

All too soon we were on the last day of our journey. This, of course, happens every year. Before we left Sackets Harbor, Sharon and I had breakfast at the same restaurant we had eaten at a couple of days before. That gave us a chance to sample a few more dishes from the menu. We were getting pretty good at waddling to our bikes and, even more impressive, we were able to get on them.

Recovery Mode

On our way into Oswego, we decided that in planning next year's trip we should to stay out of Canada. I also added to the "don't leave home without it list" a dozen screws for our bikes. I certainly was not going to ask anyone for a screw and Sharon was absolutely forbidden to even mention the word. After nine years of bicycling adventures, our vocabulary was becoming rather restricted.

**1999**
**Approximately 120 miles**

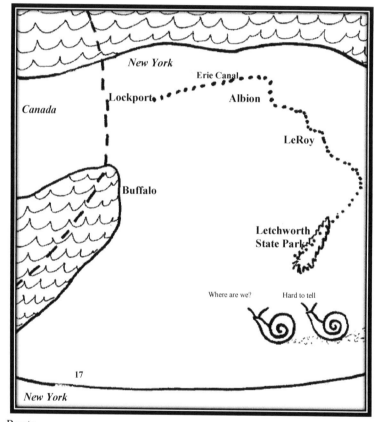

Route ...........

Highways _____

Chapter 10
1999

Buzzards, Buzzards, and more Buzzards

In 1997, for Sharon's 50<sup>th</sup> birthday, her brothers and I gave her an Alaskan cruise. Sharon's birthday is October 31, 1947. That's right ...... she was born on Halloween, which explains, in part, her personality. There is no way to explain the rest of it.

Sharon had been divorced for eleven years. Although she'd had a few serious relationships, she had not quite met the right guy. Since the cruise was for two, it was her siblings' thought that she would take her daughter, Jean. Without thinking, I had booked the cruise for September of 1998. Jean began High School that September, and there was not any practical way to take her out of school for a week without it affecting her grades and extra-curricular activities. If Jean had really wanted to go, I am sure Sharon would have arranged something with the school, but she was too excited about starting High School and had little interest in going. Sharon called me to see if I wanted to go. Let's see....would I want to go on a fully-paid cruise along the inland passage of Alaska? I couldn't wait!

While on the cruise Sharon met her future husband, Bernie Stevens. He was one of the dance hosts...but that is another story.

Sharon and Bernie had spent most of the summer of 1999 traveling across the northern part of the U.S. in their 5<sup>th</sup> wheel RV. Meanwhile, Jean was spending the summer in New York City, so before our bike trip, Sharon spent a few days visiting her. I flew into Buffalo where Bernie picked me up at the airport. We then drove to the train depot to meet Sharon, who was arriving from New York City. Once we were all gathered up, Bernie drove us to Lockport, New York.

We planned to travel on the biking paths that ran next to the old Erie Canal. The historic canal was first proposed in 1699, but construction did not begin until 1817. There was considerable opposition to the proposal. Along with the cost, which was prohibitive, the logistics seemed insurmountable. There is a 600 ft. rise from the Hudson River to Lake Erie, requiring at least 50 locks along the 360 mile

course. President Jefferson called it "a little short of madness" and rejected it.

The advocate who finally succeeded in getting the canal built was Jesse Hawley. He managed to gain the interest of New York Governor DeWitt Clinton. For years the project was debated and was soon referred to as Clinton's Folly, or Clinton's Ditch. Even today the abandoned sections are still called Clinton's Ditch. Finally, on July 4, 1817, construction of the canal began. The surveyors and engineers who supervised the construction were novices. There were no professional civil engineers in the United States at that time, but remarkably, all of the designs worked precisely as planned. The success made heroes of those whose innovations made the canal possible and led to an increased public esteem for practical education.

The Erie Canal was completed on October 26, 1825. The event was celebrated statewide, culminating in successive cannon shots along the length of the canal and the Hudson River. After only ten days of travel time from Buffalo to New York, Governor Clinton poured water from Lake Erie into New York Harbor to mark the "wedding of the waters."

The Erie Canal cut transportation costs by 95% between the western interior of America at Buffalo, and the eastern seaboard at New York City. Even as late as 1852, the canal carried thirteen times more freight than all the New York State railroads combined. As a result, the canal was the prime factor in the rise of New York City as the chief port in the U.S. Although expanded between 1834 and 1862, the original canal was replaced in 1918 by the larger New York State Barge Canal. Today the old Erie Canal System is mainly used by recreational watercraft.

August 13th

We stayed at the Hambleton House, located at 130 Pine St. in Lockport, New York. Before the creation of the Erie Canal, the area where Lockport is now located was completely undeveloped and unsettled. As soon as the construction of the canal was approved, land along the proposed route was quickly bought-up by speculators. Lockport was founded at the location of one of the locks, hence the name.

The locks were completed in 1825, and Lockport became an established village in 1829. With the completion of the canal, many of the Scottish and Irish workers stayed in Lockport, giving it the heavy Celtic influence still discernible today.

Bernie joined us for dinner at the Fieldstone Country Inn, after which he dropped us off at the B&B. The Hambleton House was very typical of many of the B&Bs we had stayed in throughout our bicycling adventures, and is still in

operation.

What I remember most about the Hambleton House was what happened in the parking lot. Wanting to get an early start the next day, Sharon and I decided to put our bikes together that evening. Since Sharon and Bernie were to meet me in Buffalo, they took both of our bikes with them for their summer tour, strapping them to the top of the fifth wheel. We did have to take them apart but certainly not to the extent that was necessary to be shipped. Only the pedals were removed and the handlebars loosened in order to lay them flat on top of the vehicle. All of our gear was packed in the RV, along with our outfits and accessories.

As we took out our tools to reassemble the bikes for the ride, it started to drizzle. While I was putting my bike together, I heard grumblings from Sharon. She had put her left pedal on and was sitting on the pavement working on the right pedal when she threw down the wrench in frustration.

"I can't get this stupid pedal to stay on," she said. When I looked up, she was slumped over, almost in tears. Seeing her so forlorn sitting in the rain was kind of sad. It was so absurd to think that after all this time it was possible we still did not know how to put our bicycles together. Okay…let us be fair. One of us still did not know how to reassemble her bike.

To Sharon's credit, however little there might be, it was raining and the parking lot was poorly lit. As soon as I saw Sharon's pathetic state, I immediately stopped what I was doing to see if I could help. She was still huddled on the ground as I took a look. Bending over her seat and peering down at her lack of progress in reattaching her pedal, I instantly saw the cause of the problem. She had successfully attached the left pedal to the left crank and had moved around to the right side to attach the right pedal. This is when she made her mistake. She was trying to put the right pedal onto the other side of the left crank which, of course, already had a pedal on it. She had managed to partially screw the right pedal onto the left crank, but not enough to keep it secure.

The sight of two pedals on one crank was too much for me. Not saying a word, I immediately started laughing, quietly though, because I knew it was a frustrating time for Sharon. But I couldn't help it. What could I say? As soon as I started to shake, the sure sign I was laughing, Sharon looked over and realized her mistake. Immediately her frustration vanished, replaced with peals of laughter, not only at herself, but also at how funny her bike looked. As we continued to work on our bikes, we would think of the two pedals on the single crank and the laughter would start all over again. We even had trouble going to sleep that night. As we lay in bed, one of us would start shaking with laughter, which would just get the other one going again.

August 14th

After breakfast, we bungeed our gear onto the bikes for the start of our new adventure. With the pedals on the correct crank and our tummies sore from laughing so much, we headed toward the Erie Canal Bikeway. We entered the bikeway at Locks 34 and 35 which we accessed off of Cold Springs Road.

This section of the bikeway is known as the Erie Canal Heritage Trail. There are four designated sections of the Canal Trail. In addition to the one we biked that year, there is the Old Erie Canal State Park, the Mohawk-Hudson Bikeway, and the Glens Falls Feeder Canal Trail. Where we entered, the trail was paved, which made for easy riding. With only 25 miles to Albion, we took our time riding along the bikeway, veering off to explore the many villages along the canal where we stopped for coffee and snacks.

As we biked along the canal, we passed a barge being towed through the water using the method of days gone by. When the canal was built, a towpath was constructed, usually on the north side. The towpath was used by horses and mules to pull the boats along. The driver of the team pulling the boat was called a "hoggee." We stopped to watch as a mule being driven by a hoggee pulled a barge along the canal. There were a couple of passengers on the boat, and everyone was dressed in period clothing. The barge passed us in a remote area with no signs of modern civilization nearby. Sharon and I, for a brief moment, were witnesses to a snapshot of history. It was quite remarkable!

We reached Albion in the early afternoon. The Friendship Inn is a beautiful old family home which, like so many such homes, had been converted into a B&B. It was common for the wealthy to build their homes on high ground. The higher on the hill a home was built, the more important the family was. Because so many of these beautiful homes had been converted into B&Bs, it was not unusual that at the end of the day we would have to ride up a hill to reach them.

Although our B&B was up a steep hill, we were not satisfied with our day's ride, having only biked 25 miles on a flat, paved bikeway. We were ready for more. Since we were leaving the canal bikeway at Albion to travel to LeRoy, we decided to spend part of the afternoon further exploring the bike path next to the canal.

After unloading our gear, we headed back to the bikeway and traveled farther east. Unfortunately, not far from where we re-entered the trail, the pavement ended. Although the trail was well-kept, chat and gravel are tough on bicycle gears and will, over time, start to jamb them. Even so, we went about another five miles along the canal before we turned around and headed back to the Friendship Inn.

That evening we ate at Navarra's family restaurant which was down the hill

from the Inn. Our third time up the hill was enough. It was time for bed, and to rest our legs for our trip to LeRoy.

August 15th

As we were preparing to leave the Friendship Inn, our hosts told us about a local fair not too far off of our route. That sounded like fun, so we decided to add the short detour to our day's ride. We headed south out of Albion on highway 98. About a mile or two outside the village, we turned north to where the fair was taking place. Not surprisingly, it was a little farther than we had been led to believe. It is always difficult for people to convert a driving distance and terrain into bicycling distance and terrain. What is close by and flat in an auto is quite often far away and hilly for a bicyclist. Once at the fair, we realized it had taken us too far out of our way to allow time for a side excursion. At the entrance, we reluctantly decided to forgo the event and continue on to LeRoy.

We were biking in the Genesee Valley, which is in the middle of some of the best agricultural land in New York. The countryside is made up of farmland and horse pastures, broken up by copses of deciduous trees.

The day was hot and humid, and the terrain was a series of rolling hills, enough of them to matter. It was nearing noon, and with still close to 40 miles ahead of us, our decision to forego the fair was proving to be insightful. My next decision was not. In studying our map I saw what looked to be a shortcut to LeRoy. In suggesting this change of plan to Sharon, I cleverly called it an alternate route. After ten years of planning our trips I had become a little smug, and therefore decided it was not necessary to reread my list on why never to take short cuts in rural areas while bicycling.

"The list"--

1. It is easy to get lost. Rural roads are not always identified. This makes it very difficult to know which road is which, and more importantly, where in the world it really goes.

2. Quite often, short cuts are not shorter. Being on bicycles, mistakes in changing your original plan actually can add enormous mileage to an already challenging day.

3. Refer to #5.

4. Weather is so unpredictable. There is always the threat of rain, thunderstorms, hurricanes, tornados, or excessive heat and humidity. None of these are welcome when you are lost.

5. Shortcuts do not always provide food opportunities when needed. Sharon is not fun to be around when she is hungry. She gets rather vicious, while showing signs of cannibalism. Snacks only go so far.

6. There are very few people nearby to ask for directions if we get lost, and rarely do cell phones work in rural areas. When we have had service and were able to call our hosts at the next B&B, it is very difficult to tell them where we are. Telling them that there are a lot of cows and corn fields has never helped in identifying our location.
7. Refer again to #5
8. There is no way to know what the terrain is like. Mountains can so easily appear from anywhere.

However, I ignored all of the wise warnings and took off down one of the country roads which wound over hill and dale. According to my map the road was to intersect Route 19 which would take us into LeRoy. Although the traffic was light, there were no shoulders. In fact, in several places the road itself was in jeopardy. The hills and dales continued on forever as the sun beat down on us with the humidity climbing…and Sharon began to look gaunt.

Somewhere, USA

Just pretending I know where we are.

 We continued on, stopping at each intersection. I couldn't tell if any of the roads we crossed were Route 19. There were no markings, which I would have known if I had glanced at #1 on my list. I chose not to tell Sharon why I was searching for road signs and studying the map so hard. My "alternate route" was devoid of towns and villages. I soon realized that I had not seen any snails, which is never a good sign. However, we did pass a lot of cows. As we passed them they would stare at us with the most confused look in their eyes, as if to ask "what are those things?" Once we passed them, they would look at each other as if to agree, "it is better that we do not mention 'those things' to the rest of the herd."

Up and down we went, passing more cows…always cows…until finally, as we headed up a long hill, we spied a tree with a large canopy at the top. We had to take a break. Even though the tree was in front of a farmhouse, the grass was just too inviting. Besides, lying around on someone's yard had never stopped us before.

The shadow of the tree was off to the left, so we were able to look up into the clear sky and still be in shadow. As we lay down, I noticed cows gathering across the road. They just lined up along the fence and stared at us. While we enjoyed the cool clover and grass, I decided to call Robert, who I had met a year and a half before.

He had known Dick in High School and, through the urging of my sister-in-law, had given me a call. Although I refused to use the word "dating", I suppose, in the real sense of the word, we were dating. As I was talking to him, I noticed several birds high in the sky. At first I thought it was my imagination or, more likely, I was suffering from heat exhaustion combined with hunger which created the illusion. As I watched, the birds were not only increasing in number, but were also starting to circle above Sharon and me. I mentioned this to Robert and he agreed that physical challenges can cause all kinds of hallucinations.

As we continued talking, the birds, which now were easily identified as buzzards and definitely not hallucinations, started to descend. It was like watching a tornado form. Dozens crowded the higher elevations. As they gathered, they began moving in a circle. The buzzards formed a funnel as they slowly circled down toward us. It was so unreal that it took a while before it dawned on me that they thought we were road kill. They had made a good call. Except for me talking on the cell phone, neither Sharon nor I had moved, and I am sure that being so sweaty, we smelled like we had long since expired.

The birds had appeared so quickly that it was very likely they had been following us, sensing the end was near. Robert couldn't believe we were being circled by buzzards and that they were closing in. I felt that it was important to inform Sharon of our predicament.

"We are being circled by buzzards," I told her. Apparently my voice had no sense of urgency since her only response was a very disinterested "should we do something?" I glanced over to see Sharon lying on her back, eyes closed, clutching a nosegay of wild flowers on her chest.

"Move", I strongly suggested. Well...that was easier said than done. We were so lethargic and sleepy it was like slow motion to get our limbs to move. I managed to shake one or two fingers and one foot which, I am afraid, the buzzards interpreted as muscle spasms that occasionally occur in the last throws of death.

On they came, closer and closer, slowly descending as they lazily circled above us. With great effort we both managed to sit up. Taking note, the buzzards reversed their circling and moved higher in the sky to wait. In the meantime, more cows gathered across the way. There was quite a herd by now. I had dropped my cell phone, but I could hear Robert laughing on the other end. Well...I was not going to include him on any bike trip!

Road Kill

With the buzzards moving higher, the immediate threat was over. Sharon and I shook ourselves awake, knowing we had better get going. No rest for the weary! Slowly, we got on our bicycles.

We were thankful we had stopped at the top of a hill. We coasted down the road, hoping the breeze would put a little energy into our efforts before we had to tackle the next hill. Whenever we stopped for a drink of water, I noticed the buzzards were still there high in the sky...watching...and waiting.

Finally we reached Route 19 which I cleverly identified by the sign that said Route 19. Thank goodness for the occasional exception to country roads being unmarked. Our much anticipated road ran along the crest of a hill overlooking the valleys. Lining the road were beautiful horse pastures with luscious, thick grass, and dotted with canopied trees. One of the farms had a number of white fences separating the pastures, which went on for miles. More than likely the owners had fox hunts, not uncommon in the Genesee Valley.

With the buzzards still in tow, we were not going to venture into any of these inviting pastures to take a break. Besides, rules #3, #5, and #7 from my list were becoming a real problem. Threats from buzzards, by the way, are not on the list. I have since added the potential threat to the list as #9.

With over ten miles to go before the next town, and now remembering #5 on the list, I kept a safe distance from Sharon, being sure to keep my arms close to my body. At the first town we came to, we headed for the nearest source of food. Once fed, Sharon and I continued on toward LeRoy, a few miles south of Interstate 90.

LeRoy, named after one of the original land owners, Herman LeRoy, was first settled in 1793. Oatka Creek flows northward through the town and was a source of water power for the early mills. LeRoy is the birthplace of Jell-O gelatin dessert and the location of the Jell-O museum. The town's main street starts on top of a hill which descends sharply down towards Oatka Creek. As we cruised down the road toward the creek and our B&B, I hoped the recommended dinner restaurants were not back up the hill.

The Hidden Garden B&B is located on the other side of the Oatka Creek, which had been dammed up to create a serene waterway, and a park had been placed along the shoreline. Our hostess recommended The Depot Restaurant for dinner. It was up the hill and off to the right...of course it would be! However, the food was worth the steep ascent back up Main Street.

August 16th

All too soon, it was our last day of our bike adventure. Our trip was to end at Letchworth State Park where once again we were to stay at the Glen Iris Inn. Bernie was to join us for our last evening.

We of course had breakfast before heading out. Upon entering the dining room, we were undone by the scrumptious delicacies already placed on the table. With no one else around, we helped ourselves to the hot coffee. On the table was a coffee ring drenched with icing. Because we were the only ones staying at the Hidden Gardens B&B, we figured the coffee ring had to be for us. We each took a piece. It was sooo delicious! We soon had to have another piece, then another.

We were just finishing the last piece of the ring when out of nowhere a

 family appeared. Unbeknownst to us, there were other guests staying at the B&B. The fact that there were a number of place settings at the table completely escaped us. With icing dripping from our lips and our month full of the remains of the coffee ring, we introduced ourselves, being sure to use our pseudonyms. Over the years these have come in handy, as you can well imagine. The family proceeded to pour their coffee and then looked around in vain for the cake they had seen us devour. Too late! Sharon and I had eaten the whole thing.

About this time, one of the hostesses appeared and we quickly apologized for eating the entire coffee ring, explaining that we had no idea that there were other guests. She just stared at the empty plate, and looked back at us, then back at the plate. The other hostess joined us and, without hesitation, grabbed the plate and said, "Oh, I will just make another." Before heading back into the kitchen she rattled off a list of breakfast selections we could choose from. They all sounded so good I think we ordered all of them, or close to it.

We were so full from breakfast that once again we found ourselves almost crawling to our bicycles upon leaving our B&B. This was happening more often since Sharon and I now choose our B&B based not only on location, but also on breakfast menus, if available. However, we did not leave the Hidden Gardens without getting the recipe for the coffee ring. Before we headed out, we took time to enjoy the park by the Oakta Creek. We were too full to even think about bicycling anywhere.

We had a thirty mile trip to Letchworth. The weather was pretty much like the day before. I made a mental note that I would not suggest a "short cut."

Because it was hot and humid, we made a number of stops to replenish our liquids. Sharon and I have developed a great drink, perfect for replenishing the electrolytes that are always escaping. We combine PowerAde with Emergen-C.

As we rode along we kept a sharp eye out for buzzards, but didn't see any. We hoped by now they were seeking other prey. We traveled through some beautiful, picturesque countryside along tree lined streams, idyllic horse pastures, and farms.

In previous years, we had always entered Letchworth from the west and south end where the Glen Iris is located. This time we came from the north which allowed us to travel the full length of the park, seeing much of it for the first time. The road through Letchworth is rather narrow and not particularly recommended for bicycling because cars have to pass so close to the riders.

Bernie caught up to us soon after we entered the park and stopped to pick us up. We flatly refused since we wanted to enjoy our last few miles before ending our trip for another year. Or could it have been that, in returning to where our journeys had first begun, for old time's sake we wanted to follow rule #5 just one more time? We waved Bernie on but not before we asked him to have a beer ready for our arrival.

When we rode up to the Glen Iris we saw him sitting on the veranda, enjoying his beer, with two others already poured for us. Sharon and I had come back to where it all started ten years before. As we sat on the porch listening to the cascading Middle Falls, we looked at each other, raised our glasses to silently give thanks, and to toast ten wonderful years of misadventures. What a journey! For the briefest of moments, I was sure I saw Shannon and Ouisi with glasses held high.

**Shannon    Sharon    Clayton    Ouisi**

# EPILOGUE

**With another ten years of misadventures, Sharon and I *Had to Take Another Break*. Look for the sequel in 2013.**

In our next book you, will find out why trying to feed the masses makes it difficult to leave Canada.